Praise for
The Cybersecurity Spiral of Failure

. . . .

I blinked when JC Gaillard reminded us that the role of CISO was initiated in the late 90s. We must not stand still. Cyber evolves and so must we. The *'Cybersecurity Spiral of Failure'* openly explores and challenges leadership, management and governance matters to address the real dynamics of security transformation. This is a must read for anyone looking to turn their cyber practice around.

**Avril Chester |
Award-winning Technology Entrepreneur & CTO**

JC deconstructs with great accuracy how corporate short-termism and an excessive focus on purely technical approaches have failed to deliver adequate protection from cyber threats; an original and genuine book that takes a step back from the traditional tech clichés on the topic and truly puts things in perspective around cybersecurity.

**Nick Evans |
Founder, Thinkers360**

A refreshing outlook on the cybersecurity corporate landscape from a really independent and authentic voice in the industry. In 'The Cybersecurity Spiral of Failure', JC Gaillard truly reaches beyond the technology horizon into the dynamics of execution and transformation in large organizations. A must-read for the C suite.

**Henk van der Heijden |
Former Global Head of Portfolio Security
Services, Getronics**

JC and I have worked together for many years and his vision around what is going wrong in the cybersecurity industry is spot on; we have been looking at it from a purely technical perspective for over two decades while this is in fact about people and process first; anybody interested in getting a grip on their cybersecurity challenges must read this.

**Jeremy Hill |
Former Head of Identity and Access Management,
Euroclear, Refinitiv, Lloyds Banking Group**

'The Cybersecurity Spiral of Failure' is a refreshing take on cybersecurity. JC breaks down the flaws in traditional approaches, urging a shift from technology-first to governance and culture. The book addresses boardroom mistakes, the skills gap, and highlights the need for a new CISO profile with a focus on leadership and innovation. JC's insights on automation, budgets, and a lasting transformation provide practical advice. In a nutshell, it's a must-read for a practical, strategic approach to cybersecurity challenges.

Natasha McCabe |
Global Head of Corporate Technology, Schroders

JC provides a comprehensive view of the challenges faced in the cybersecurity domain and thoughtfully suggests a way forward. It is a must-read for anyone vested in this crucial aspect of business in our digital world. He delves deep into the complexities of the cybersecurity landscape, tracing its evolution over two decades. With a compelling narrative, JC emphasises the paradox of short-term fixes and the box-ticking culture among executives, which has been fuelling the short tenure of CISOs. Many, he argues, have remained technologists and firefighters, disconnected from the board's increasing focus on resilience and execution. JC's central thesis is the need for trust between CISOs and senior executives, and he makes a strong case for operational successes to foster trust and commitment from top management. Overall, a great read.

Tony Moroney |
Top 10 Digital Disruption & Top 25 Digital
Transformation by Thinkers 360
(@BetaMoroney)

This is a long-overdue diagnostic on twenty years of corporate failures around cybersecurity. Industry expert and top strategic advisor JC Gaillard addresses without complacency and in plain language the cultural and governance issues that have prevented large organizations to protect themselves from cyber threats, and more importantly, highlights a clear and visionary way forward. An essential read for any top executive on cybersecurity.

Andrew Pryor |
Founder & Director, CIO Water Cooler

Many cybersecurity practitioners will recognize page after page the situations JC describes in this book. This is a long-awaited - and at times painfully accurate - real life assessment of the corporate dynamics that have surrounded cybersecurity for the last two decades in large firms.

Daniel Sergile, CISSP |
Senior Director – Transformation,
Palo Alto Networks Unit42

The Cybersecurity Spiral of Failure

(and How to Break Out of It)

Why large firms still struggle with cybersecurity and how to engineer real change dynamics

Jean-Christophe Gaillard

Leaders
Press

ISBN 978-1-63735-249-6 (paperback)
ISBN 978-1-63735-010-2 (ebook)

Library of Congress Control Number: 2023922954

Contents

· ·

Foreword

· ·

Cybersecurity is Not Working: Time to Try Something Else

I think it is time to accept that the role of the CISO, in its historical construction, was never born out of a positive and proactive management decision.

It was very rarely created – at first – in response to the true realization by senior management of the need to protect the business from real and active threats.

The original iteration of the role, in the late nineties for the early adopters, belongs to that first decade of infosec, which was entirely dominated by risk and compliance considerations: The Security Transformation Research Foundation established this quite clearly through its 2019 semantic analysis of the content of 17 annual Global Security Reports from EY (STRF, 2019).

Information security was simply seen by senior executives as a constant balancing act between regulatory compliance, risk appetite, and – above all – costs.

The role of the CISO appeared in that context at best in response to audit or regulatory observations, at worst, at their imposition, and almost as a necessary evil in some cases.

Of course, the role has evolved since then, but an entire generation of security practitioners has been trapped in a bottom-up mindset, always in search of ways to justify its legitimacy towards the business.

This is amply demonstrated by the endless debate around the CISO's reporting line, and in particular the obsession of some with a board-level reporting, or the evolution of the role in some firms towards IT Risk or Information Risk constructions, attached to a broader Enterprise or Operational Risk function.

Generally, those moves, all well-intentioned and aimed at broadening the acceptance of necessary security measures across the firm, have rarely worked to a full extent.

Over two decades, those bottom-up approaches have collided with endemic corporate short-termism and dysfunctional corporate governance practices and have failed to deliver essential levels of good practice, and to protect against constantly evolving threats, as demonstrated by the endless string of cyberattacks we are witnessing today.

All this has left many CISOs frustrated and is fuelling their short tenure, short tenure which – by itself – has become the root cause of the long-term stagnation of cybersecurity maturity in many firms.

But now, in addition, the agenda is shifting at board level. Cyberattacks are increasingly seen as a matter of 'when', not 'if', weakening all lines of discussions that have tried over the years – bottom-up – to talk about cybersecurity in terms of risk and bringing it closer to corporate risk practices in a quest for legitimacy.

Risk is about things that may or may not happen; it can be accepted, transferred, mitigated.

The 'when, not if' paradigm around cyberattacks pushes the debate into a different dimension.

And many CISOs are not really prepared when the dialogue with top executives shifts overnight from 'why do we need to do this?' to 'how much do we need to spend?'.

This is no longer about 'convincing' them about an alleged 'return-on-security-investment', but about getting things done, and getting them done now.

But many CISOs, changing jobs every two years or so, have not learnt to get things done in large firms; they have not developed the political acumen and the management experience they would need.

Many have simply remained technologists and firefighters, trapped in an increasingly obsolete mindset, pushing bottom-up a tools-based, risk-based, tech-driven narrative, disconnected from what the board wants to hear which has now shifted towards resilience and execution.

This is why we may have to come to the point where we have to accept that the construction around the role of the CISO, as it was initiated in the late 90s, has served its purpose and needs to evolve.

The first step in this evolution, in my opinion, is for the board to own cybersecurity as a business problem, not as a technology problem.

It needs to be owned at board level in business terms, in line with the way other topics are owned at board level. This is about thinking the protection of the business in business terms, not in technology terms.

Cybersecurity is not a purely technological matter; it has never been and cannot be. The successful protection of the business from cyber threats requires to reach across corporate silos, including IT of course, but also business and support functions and geographies.

There may be a need to amalgamate it with other matters such as corporate resilience, business continuity or data privacy to build up a suitable board-level portfolio, but for me this is the way forward in reversing the long-term dynamics, away from the failed historical bottom-up constructions, towards a progressive top-down approach.

I refute the idea that board members would not have the necessary skills to drive a meaningful top-down engagement around a subject as specific as cybersecurity.

To me, this is just a remnant and the last line of defence of the tech-focused bottom-up spirit that has been dominating for over two decades.

Board members may not have the skills to drive a top-down engagement in the way bottom-up engagements have been framed for the past twenty years, but that doesn't mean that they would not be able to comprehend the matter, owning it and driving it at their level and in their own terms – possibly with some external assistance.

The hard reality is that the technology-focused bottom-up approaches most have been pushing for twenty years around cybersecurity have not worked.

It is simply time to try something else.

JC Gaillard
October 2023

Introduction

· ·

Trust between CISOs and senior executives is the only platform on which successful transformative efforts can be built around cybersecurity.

For the past two decades, many organizations have been trapped in a spiral of failure around cybersecurity, driven by endemic business short-termism and the box-ticking culture of many executives around compliance.

Cybersecurity is a complex matter that needs to reach a long way out of its native technical niche, towards business and support functions, and across geographies.

Successful transformation in that space takes time because of the need to reach across those, and effectively embed secure practices across the culture of the firm.

In real life, many senior executives struggle with a genuine long-term view. *'In the long-term we are all dead'* and many CISOs coming up with multi-year transformative plans would have been forced by their bosses to focus tactically on alleged quick-wins and compliance box-ticking measures to get their plans accepted, before seeing their initiatives deprioritized at the first sign of any business development (merger, acquisition, arrival or departure of senior executives, economic downturn or anything else)

All this has been fuelling the short tenure of CISOs and the succession of cybersecurity leaders – each coming in with their own priorities, pet subjects and pet products – simply led, in many firms, to an accumulation of poorly-deployed, under-utilized 'solutions', invariably architected around the specific capabilities of individual technical tools.

This proliferation of technical debt has reached colossal proportions, with a recent TrendMicro survey (amongst others) suggesting that 'global organizations have on average 29 security monitoring solutions in place' (TrendMicro, 2021).

It breeds a level of operational complexity which is highly expensive to run, but also talent-attritive due to the inherently manual nature of the processes it creates; we have reached a point where many security practices have become impossible to scale up in their current state due to the ongoing tensions on the skills market.

SOC analysts burn out; breaches keep happening and senior executives develop a sense that cybersecurity is just a cost and a problem, which compounds their distrust and reluctance to commit resources (in the face of endemic execution failure in that space), and their native short-termist and box-ticking tendencies (in the face of endless incidents and the regulatory pressure that situation brings).

Many CISOs think this is a cycle that has to be broken at the top, by convincing the business of the value of cybersecurity to unlock strategic long-term dynamics.

This is the line of thought that has produced endless material over the past two decades about 'cybersecurity-as-an-enabler' and 'return-on-security-investment'.

This is often a very hard line to follow in practice, as it generally pitches the CISO (bottom-up) against deeply-rooted business mindsets, and dysfunctional practices which (almost always) span a long way further than cybersecurity: Do not expect cybersecurity governance to work well, in an organization where corporate governance is broken; do not expect cybersecurity projects to deliver, in an organization where projects don't deliver... Those are not problems the CISOs on their own can address.

In my experience, this complex endeavour often leads to nowhere, aggravating further the short tenure of CISOs.

CISOs may encounter more success tackling the problem at operational level and prove their worth by making cybersecurity work for the firm, reducing operational complexity, bringing costs under control, improving on analysts retention (and mental health), and ultimately, showing that an effective and efficient security operational practice does prevent breaches.

Dealing with the cybersecurity technical debt will invariably involve working at a number of levels:

- Focusing on process and people first, to kill the dynamics and the culture by which buying more technical tools is the answer to any security problem (in spite of what vendors would like you to believe);

- Decluttering the existing cybersecurity technical estate by streamlining operational processes and removing useless legacy layers;

- Focusing security automation of improving the efficiency of analysts by removing or simplifying manual tasks, so that they can dedicate more time to the higher value jobs for which they were trained and hired (incident management or threat intelligence for example).

This is also about turning cybersecurity from a problem and a cost, into a success story: A positive force that protects the business – effectively and efficiently.

Trust between CISOs and senior executives is the only platform on which successful transformative efforts can be built around cybersecurity.

Operational success should breed trust, and trust should bring management attention and resources beyond the immediate horizon.

Those are the themes we will be exploring in the following sections.

They frame the structure of the spiral of failure that has been developing around cybersecurity over the last decades and offer directions to break out of it.

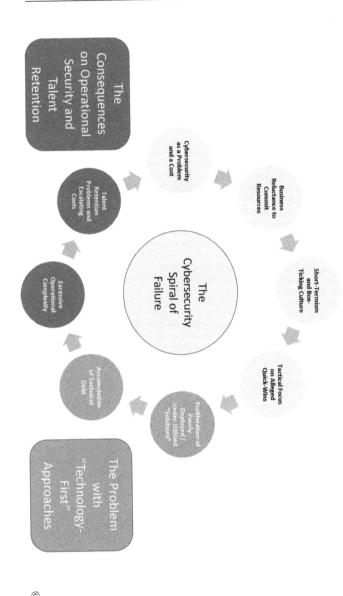

The Problem with the Historical Business Perspective on Cybersecurity

The Consequences on Operational Security and Talent Retention

Cybersecurity as a Problem and a Cost

Business Reluctance to Commit Resources

Talent Retention Problems and Escalating Costs

The Cybersecurity Spiral of Failure

Short-Termism and Box-Ticking Culture

Excessive Operational Complexity

Tactical Focus on Alleged Quick-Wins

Accumulation of Technical Debt

Proliferation of Poorly-Deployed / Under-Utilized "Solutions"

The Problem with "Technology-First" Approaches

1

The Problem with the Historical Business Perspective on Cybersecurity

. . . .

Only a Cultural Shift across the Boardroom Can Move the Needle

The cybersecurity survey released by BT Security in January 2021 is interesting, if only by the size of the population surveyed (over seven thousand people) and its triple focus on consumers, employees, and business leaders. (BT, 2021) (HelpNetSecurity, Major trends that are changing the CISO role, 2021)

But its findings are problematic – in particular in what they reveal about the attitude of senior executives towards cybersecurity and the persistence of some problems at the top.

It starts well, with some stats broadly consistent with other surveys and anecdotal field evidence: 58 percent saying that improving data and network security has become more important to their organisation in the last year and 76 percent rating their organisations as 'good' or 'excellent' at protecting itself from cyber threats.

But these stats are hard to reconcile with others in the report. On page 7, they mention that 'fewer than one third of business leaders rate key components of their company's IT security as excellent' and that, broadly, they have 'low confidence in the organisation's ability to deliver the fundamentals.' Also, page 13 mentions the statement that 'fewer than half of executives and employees can put a name to their CISO.'

Without fuller access to the underlying data set, it is hard to draw hard conclusions beyond the fact that, clearly, an amount of confusion persists among business leaders around cybersecurity. How can you say that security is becoming more important, and your organisation is well protected and at the same time be unable to name your CISO? And what does that tell us about the profile of the CISOs in those organisations?

Another aspect, typical of those surveys, is the emphasis on getting the security basics right and the importance of awareness development among employees.

To truly move the needle on those matters, you need to go beyond the obvious and start confronting the real underlying issues. This is something on which we already commented in 2020, in relation to several reports from the World Economic Forum. (CorixPartners, 2020)

Of course, getting the basics right and training employees are essential pillars of any cybersecurity practice, but the real question remains:

Why are we still here banging about it?

Good cybersecurity practices, such as those mentioned in the BT survey (patching, access management, etc.) have been regarded as good practices for the best part of the last two decades, and large organisations that, collectively, would have spent tens or hundreds of millions on cybersecurity across that period should not be in such poor state. Period.

The underlying causes of that failure are rooted in adverse prioritisation by the business, short-termism, and internal politics. All factors point firmly towards problems of culture and governance at the top.

Until surveys such as this one, or earlier ones from the World Economic Forum for example (WEF, 2019) (WEF, 2020), start tackling those issues, not much will move for good around cybersecurity.

The same can be said broadly around security awareness development. Of course, it's essential … but the 'human firewall' has to start at the top of the organisation.

How can you expect staff to follow good practices and accept security constraints if they see senior executives constantly allowed to skip the rules?

There is so much a CISO and their organisation can push horizontally across the business or from the bottom up, and without a clear and unambiguous endorsement from the top, the best cybersecurity awareness programme can quickly turn into an expensive box-checking exercise ... The example must come consistently from the top for any security awareness programme to stick and yield results.

So the CISOs are indeed 'under the spotlight,' but can they really 'drive the reset' induced by the 'speed and scale of the digital transformation triggered by the global pandemic' (page 13)?

In the current state of affairs, probably not.

The attitude senior executives have had towards security in most organisations over the past two decades has driven towards CISO roles a certain type of people. Most are technologists, consultants, or auditors by background; very few come from true business roles.

So before the CISO can 'drive the reset,' it is the role itself that needs a reset. 'Enterprises urgently need to elevate cybersecurity leadership' (page 13).

On that point, the BT survey is spot on. But it is easier said than done.

Once again, this is something that has to come from the top, and it may require a broadening of the traditional CISO portfolio towards continuity and privacy, effectively building up the role into an elevated CSO role able to reach across the organisation.

Such shift, supported at board level and coupled with adequate compensation packages and career profiling, should attract a different type of executive and drive change. This is the type of move we have been advocating since 2018 to address the challenges of the digital transformation and the increased demands on privacy compliance that came with GDPR (CorixPartners, 2018).

But going back to the BT survey, to fix all this and get cybersecurity moving for good, you need to tackle the problem at board level, not at CISO level.

It is only a cultural shift across the boardroom that will move the needle.

The Three Biggest Mistakes the Board Can Make around Cybersecurity

The role of the board in relation to cybersecurity is a topic I have written about several times since 2015, first in the wake of the TalkTalk data breach in the United Kingdom (CorixPartners, 2015) (CorixPartners, 2016), then in 2019 following the WannaCry and NotPeyta outbreaks and data breaches at BA, Marriott, and Equifax among others (CorixPartners, 2019), and even more recently in response to an article in the Harvard Business Review (HBR, 7 Pressing Cybersecurity Questions Boards Need to Ask, 2022) (CorixPartners, 2022). This is also a topic we have been researching with techUK, and that collaboration resulted in the start of their Cyber People series (techUK, 2021).

Overall, although the topic of cybersecurity is now definitely on the board's agenda in most organisations, it is rarely a fixed item. More often than not, it makes appearances at the request of the audit and risk committee, after a question from a non-executive director or, worse, in response to a security incident or a near-miss.

All this hides a pattern of recurrent cultural and governance attitudes that could be hindering cybersecurity more than enabling it.

There are three big mistakes the board needs to avoid to promote cybersecurity and prevent breaches.

1. Downgrading It: 'We Have Bigger Fishes to Fry.'

Of course, each organisation is different, and the COVID crisis, for example, would have affected many differently – from those nearing collapse, to those that were booming.

But pretending that the protection of the business from cyber threats is not a relevant board topic now borders on negligence and is certainly a matter of poor governance that non-executive directors have a duty to pick up.

Cyberattacks are in the news every week and have been the direct cause of millions in direct losses and hundreds of millions in lost revenues in many large organisations across almost all industry sectors.

Data privacy regulators have suffered setbacks over recent years. They have been forced to adjust down some of their fines (BA, Marriott), and we have also seen a first successful challenge in Austria leading to a multimillion fine being overturned (€18 million for Austrian Post). Nevertheless, fines are now reaching the millions or tens of millions regularly. It is still very far from the 4 percent of global turnover allowed under the GDPR, but the upwards trend is clear (as DLA Piper keeps highlighting in their annual GDPR survey) (DLAPiper, 2023), and those numbers should register on the radar of most boards.

Finally, the COVID crisis has made most businesses heavily dependent on digital services, the stability of which is built on sound cybersecurity practices, in-house and across the supply chain.

Cybersecurity has become a pillar of the 'new normal' and, even more than before, should be a regular board agenda, clearly visible in the portfolio of one member who should have part of their remuneration linked to it (should remuneration practices allow). As stated above, this is fast becoming a plain matter of good governance.

2. Seeing It as an IT Problem: 'IT Is Dealing with This.'

This is a dangerous stance at a number of levels.

First, cybersecurity has never been a purely technological matter. The protection of the business from cyber threats has always required concerted action at people, process, and technology levels across the organisation.

Reducing it to a tech matter downgrades the subject, and as a result, the calibre of talent it attracts. In large organisations that are intrinsically territorial and political, it has led to an endemic failure to address cross-silo issues for decades (e.g., around identity or vendor risk management) in spite of the millions spent on those matters with tech vendors and consultants.

So it should not be left to the CIO to deal with, unless their profile is sufficiently elevated within the organisation.

In the past, we have advocated alternative organisational models to address the challenges of the digital transformation and the necessary reinforcement of practices around data privacy in the wake of the GDPR. They remain current and, of course, are not meant to replace the 'three lines of defence' type of models.

But here again, caution should prevail. It is easy – in particular in large firms – to overengineer the three lines of defence and to build monstrous, inefficient control models. The three lines of defence can only work on trust, and they must bring visible value to each part of the control organisation to avoid creating a culture of suspicion and regulatory window dressing (CorixPartners, 2017).

3. Throwing Money at It: 'How Much Do We Need to Spend to Get this Fixed?'

The protection of the business from cyber threats is something you need to grow, not something you can buy – in spite of what countless tech vendors and consultants would like you to believe.

As a matter of fact, most of the breached organisations of the past few years – BA, Marriott, Equifax, Travelex, Colonial, etc. (the list is long) – would have spent collectively tens or hundreds of millions on cybersecurity products over the last decades.

Where cybersecurity maturity is low and profound transformation is required, simply throwing money at the problem is rarely the answer.

Of course, investments will be required, but the real silver bullets are to be found in corporate culture, corporate governance, and the true embedding of business protection values in the corporate purpose. It is something that needs to start at the top of the organisation through visible and credible board ownership of those issues and cascade down through middle management, relayed by incentives and remuneration schemes.

This is more challenging than doing ad hoc pen tests, but it is the only way to lasting long-term success.

What Cyber Resilience Is Not About

Although the theme is gaining momentum, there is a certain amount of confusion around what cyber resilience really means for organisations. For many, it is just another piece of consultant jargon, an abstract managerial concept with little real life substance or meaning.

As a matter of fact, it is very real, and it is rooted in the 'when, not if' paradigm around cyberattacks, which is completely changing the dynamics around cybersecurity in many firms.

At the heart of cyber resilience lies a real application of 'defence-in-depth' principles that have been well established for decades: acting at preventative, detective, mitigative, and reactive levels – and across the real breadth of the enterprise, functionally and geographically. It is about the enterprise being enabled by the use of data and technology, while remaining protected from active threats.

It requires managerial and governance practices to be active across corporate silos and the supply chain (once again, functionally and geographically), and it cannot be dissociated from a broader approach to operational and corporate resilience.

It is hard to deliver at scale, and it presents many large organisations with significant cultural challenges. So the temptation is high for many to oversimplify it and focus only on alleged quick wins.

Of course, the 'when, not if' paradigm implies that security breaches are unavoidable. But it does not represent a licence to ignore all protective, detective, and mitigative measures to focus only on the reactive ones. This is the type of simplistic approach to 'resilience' that may put a few ticks in audit or compliance boxes, but in the long term, it can only aggravate security postures and lead to regulatory issues – in particular in the face of a worldwide tightening of regulations around the protection of personal data.

'Cyber resilience' cannot be limited to an annual desktop exercise with board members and corporate functions, during which they simulate how to react to a cyberattack, in order to minimise the impact on the share price, media coverage, or the reactions of customers.

All those factors are important, but 'cyber resilience' must not turn into an excuse to legitimise a top-down window dressing culture around cybersecurity practices.

Corporate resilience is the ability of an organisation to continue operating in the face of disruptive events and to return to stable operations over time. It implies a deep knowledge of operational processes, their integration, and their interdependencies. It also implies a deep knowledge of the supply chain and its actors.

To operate efficiently in disrupted situations, it also requires a collaborative and positive culture that needs to be created and fostered from the top down.

All this is even more acute in cyber resilience scenarios due to their relative novelty, the speed at which the organisation often needs to react, and the technical complexity that may be involved.

Instead of being treated as another box-checking exercise and a quick win, cyber resilience must be embedded into the right corporate structures and used to channel a different culture from the top down around cybersecurity:

- A culture where cybersecurity (the need to protect the business from cyber threats) and the protection of individuals' privacy are not just matters of risk management or necessary evils imposed by compliance and regulations but key business concepts and, increasingly, matters of competitive advantage and corporate social responsibility.

- A culture that fosters the transversal nature of many security problems in large firms (looking across corporate is certainly much beyond the mere technology horizon), because the security measures needed to protect the firm are transversal in nature. Their execution is the only factor that will protect the business, and it requires transversal capabilities.

- Finally, a culture rooted in transparency around security breaches, because trust is the cornerstone of the digital economy and transparency is its foundation.

Cybersecurity and the Incoming CIO: What's Really Going On?

Here is a scenario we are seeing far too often in the field:

A new CIO comes in, identifies security problems, then nothing serious happens.

At best, some tactical initiative would be pushed forward to answer outstanding audit issues, or a big gun of the industry would be called in to deliver countless slides, out of which some hypothetical 'quick wins' would be enacted to calm the board about cyber risks.

Why so many incoming CIOs seem to be so cautious on cybersecurity at the early stages of their tenure, in the face of glaring internal issues and constant reminders of data breaches in the news, is a worrying question. Their answers are invariably the same:

- They have more pressing problems elsewhere.
- They have bigger fishes to fry.
- The business won't wear it.
- The budgets are too tight.
- A new organisation is due to be announced 'next week' or 'next month.'
- They'll 'come to it' in due course, 'next year,' or 'once the new CEO has decided where priorities should be.'

In most large firms, these have to be seen as poor excuses. The CIO would often have hundreds of staff in their teams, tens of millions in annual budget, and a significant direct sign-off limit consistent with their board-level reporting line.

In a context where everything runs in parallel and everything costs money, the truth is that addressing cybersecurity shortcomings from the start is often a mere matter of priorities for any new CIO – priorities and personal courage. The reality is that the underlying security problems are invariably complex and involve a combination of organisational, technical, and managerial issues:

- Legacy InfoSec teams buried in the org chart, poorly staffed, poorly skilled, and forced into constant tactical and technical firefighting.

- Expensive technical security initiatives half deployed and poorly sold to business and IT staff because they were always designed as point solutions to specific problems in the absence of any bigger picture and, as a result, perceived as a burden and a waste of money.

- Senior management very willing to accept cyber risk as a top risk for the firm but, at the same time, themselves refusing to adhere to basic rules of security hygiene when it comes to mobile devices or passwords (rules that they are otherwise happy to impose on all other members of the staff).

Standing up to the board on those matters to tell them what they need to have, not just give them what they want, takes some gravitas but should elevate the role of the CIO, not diminish it. For most large and complex firms, if cybersecurity maturity is low because nothing structured has ever been done in that space in the past, a data breach is merely a question of time. And given current levels of media and political interest on these topics, gambling on it could be costly in a number of ways (financially or reputationally for the firm, personally for the CEO), as amply demonstrated at least in the United Kingdom since the TalkTalk data breach in 2015.

Not only is waiting for something to happen a dangerous game, but it often leads to absurd knee-jerk reactions that simply perpetuate the pre-existing short-termist approach to security without creating any fundamental change momentum.

Incoming CIOs should not be scared to launch into a cybersecurity transformation programme at the early stages of their tenure if they see a need, and good governance around cybersecurity is fast becoming 'the most important criterion for an organisation to feel well protected,' as highlighted as early as 2016 by a short survey from recruitment firm Boyden collating feedback from thirty-six top CIOs (Boyden, 2016).

Of course, there may be legacy people problems to resolve, and these may take time, but overall, building a sound security organisation and operating model able to reach and operate across the whole firm is often the best start. Many security problems cut across corporate silos (into HR, legal, and business disciplines), and a strong CISO with true management experience – not a mere firefighter or a technology hobbyist – can be a strong ally for the CIO in broader transformational battles across IT or the business.

The Two Factors Killing GRC Practices

Many CISOs complain of communication problems with their business. They are not being listened to. They are not getting the budget they think they should get. They feel their business prioritises against security too often.

It has been a recurring theme among information security professionals for the best part of the last fifteen years, and it is rooted in a wide range of factors, among which the profile of the CISO is often a dominant limitation.

Many CISOs are simply too technical. They know they need to bridge the gap with their business, but they often return to their comfort zone at the first opportunity. For them, 'threats' are often translated into malware, phishing, and hackers, while the business wants to hear insider fraud or intellectual property theft.

This often leads to the CISO role being ring-fenced and limited to its first-line technical remit, while GRC functions develop in the second line of defence. But those functions themselves very often struggle to develop meaningful conversations with their business around cybersecurity.

GRC teams tend to have an ivory-towered view of the problem and rely on ready-made, overly complex methodologies loosely related to the reality of first-line activities.

They rush into buying some tech platform that is supposed to 'enable' the GRC process, but in reality, the jargon of those products and methodologies is often meaningless to the business. Impact assessments and risk assessments can be inextricably complex. The quality of the data collected is often questionable as a result, and many of those approaches never scale up for good in large firms due to the sheer human cost of deploying them.

The lack of hard-wiring for first-line activities makes the GRC metrics produced artificial and unusable in practice to recommend, justify, or manage the first-line investment. If, in addition, the scope covered is limited due to deployment or acceptance issues, the overall value of such metrics can be highly disputable – beyond the proverbial 'tick-in-the-box' that they will invariably provide.

Overall, excessive complexity and lack of first-Line integration render many GRC metrics useless.

None of that helps the business understand and manage its cyber risk posture. Over time, distrust sets in, and as the 'when, not if' paradigm around cyberattacks takes root in the boardroom, senior executives need to find a way out.

It can only involve refocusing GRC practices towards simplicity so they can be effectively and efficiently deployed on a large scale across the real breadth of the firm – and possibly towards its supply chain.

It will also involve refocusing GRC practices towards a proper and meaningful integration with first-line cybersecurity data so that GRC metrics reflect the reality of the first line of defence.

The 'when, not if' paradigm makes the board increasingly willing to invest to ensure the protection of the firm from cyber threats, but it also shifts priorities towards measuring progress and ensuring things get done.

In many firms, the equation between governance, risk, and compliance around cybersecurity is becoming heavily weighted towards the G, and GRC functions must adjust as a result, both in terms of internal structures and in terms of interactions with other stakeholders.

In particular, the first line and second line must work together on this. They must trust each other and look beyond absurd and arbitrary 'separation of duties' concepts to produce meaningful data for the business, around which meaningful decisions will be made to protect the firm.

A Reality Check Around Cybersecurity Benchmarking

For as long as I have been involved in cybersecurity, I have heard top executives asking for benchmarking data around their cybersecurity practice.

It might have been in terms of maturity, security spending, or frequency of breaches, but 'how are the others doing' has always been a fairly common question.

I think this goes way beyond 'herd mentality', and context is key to position the right answer, so before going any further, CISOs facing that type of situation must ask themselves where the concern is coming from.

If the question is coming up in a context of budgetary or strategic orientations discussions, it often reflects a need for re-assurance, if not plain discomfort, with regards to what is being proposed.

Top executives should know that each organisation is different, even across the same industry (many would have built their careers moving from one firm to another across that spectrum).

They should also understand that differences in cyber maturity and risk appetite can drive different approaches, and that organisations don't easily share sufficient quantitative data at that level to allow meaningful comparisons: They – themselves – may not be comfortable seeing disclosed to competitors how much they are budgeting for cybersecurity for example.

The objective could be to drive the CISO's ambitions up or down, but in most cases, the benchmarking question is politically loaded, and it has never been a simple one to answer quantitatively with any degree of accuracy.

Most CISOs have historically tried to address it in a qualitative manner based on anecdotal evidence gathered at conferences or through industry forums, but window-dressing a few anecdotal data points to make them look bigger than they are can be a dangerous and misleading game.

Only a small number of very large management consulting firms might have the necessary elements of data – or the reach to collect it; but even that reach is likely to be limited to the large firms able to afford their services, and they will have to anonymise or aggregate the findings to respect the confidentiality of their clients.

CISOs might be better off in many cases by sidestepping the question: For most firms, there is simply no defendable, sufficiently accurate, quantitative answer to the cybersecurity benchmarking question.

CISOs should focus instead on the underlying motivation of the senior executives behind the question.

Trust between them is of paramount importance to any transformative initiative around cybersecurity, and the benchmarking question could be symptom of trust erosion.

That's a far more serious matter to address than the collection of illusory comparative data.

Trust – at this level – will have its foundations in mutual respect and that has to start for the CISO by listening to the real priorities and constraints of the leadership team, and understanding the implications these may have on cybersecurity orientations, for good or for bad.

They will have to elevate their game to look convincingly beyond the tech horizon and showcase their understanding of the key governance and management matters at the heart of the cross-functional nature of cybersecurity in large firms.

As the 'when, not if' paradigm around cyberattacks becomes prevalent across the boardroom, CISOs must also focus their attention on demonstrating their long-term ability to execute on transformative measures and stop relying only on their short-term firefighting skills to build up their case.

It is likely that benchmarking will cease to be concern for senior executives if they have the sense cybersecurity is in firm hands and driven in a direction that matches their expectations and the needs of the firm.

The Cybersecurity Numbers Game is a Dangerous One for CISOs

Which vendor cybersecurity survey are we meant to believe?

This one – from Panaseer – arguing that CISOs would require a 40 percent increase in their budgets to be confident to mitigate security risks? (HelpNetSecurity, 2023)

Or this one – from Expel – stating that 26.7 percent of security budgets were left unspent in 2022 in the UK? (BusinessWire, 2023)

Let's start by repeating the obvious: This is vendor-led content, more than 'proper' research. Those surveys claim to analyse results from hundreds of respondents – and those numbers are probably true – but little analytics is generally applied to the data beyond the calculation of percentages and the commentaries alongside the data are always tainted by the views of the sponsors and the potential use cases of their products.

They should be seen as indicators, nothing else; but they often match an amount of anecdotal evidence we collect in the field regularly.

In fact, those two surveys don't really contradict each other, but they certainly paint a contrasted picture, and it feels strange that the CISOs asking for more money could be the same who actually struggle to spend it.

It might sound counter-intuitive, but I think that the CISOs struggling to spend it are more likely to be the – rare – ones who did get that large budgetary increase in their last round.

There is no doubt in my opinion that a vast proportion of security budgets in large firms is used to prop-up legacy processes, and the monumental technical debt of security estates built around countless tools. Toolkit consolidation is a necessity in large firms: They simply cannot continue to operate the bloated security estates and manual processes of the past, given the current constraints on skills, the mounting regulatory pressure and the constant escalation of threats.

It is a mistake to think that this can be solved quickly and simply by throwing more money at the situation.

Transformative efforts need resources of course, but they also need time, vision, and drive. And support from above in manners that exceed budgetary commitments because cybersecurity is, by essence, cross-functional.

This is where many CISOs go wrong in building up their case towards decision makers: They think this is a rational argument, to be won with facts, data and numbers.

This is the school of thought that has led to the creation of countless security ROI and cost-cutting models, and some of those models might have served their purpose in some situations: After all, they offer the appearance of science and being visible at spending around cybersecurity protects top executives; it puts ticks in the right boxes with auditors and regulators – at a time where personal liability is becoming a top concern for many – and if breaches keep happening, execution failures can be blamed on the CISO who becomes the natural scapegoat.

Without realising it, CISOs playing that sort of numbers game often end up weakened and exposed.

In fact, even when taking up a new job and finding a clear legacy of underspending and underbudgeting, CISOs must not start by asking themselves 'how do I justify spending more' but 'where does that situation come from'.

Long-term battles with top executives are not fought and won in the field of numbers. They belong to a different terrain.

The real long-term currency here is the trust between the CISO and the rest of the leadership team.

And it has to start by the CISO listening to all stakeholders, their constraints, their problems and their priorities – instead of telling them upfront what they're doing wrong and what needs fixing, always pushing a technical agenda.

With trust as its foundation, the dialogue between the CISO and stakeholders acquires a different dimension.

Top executives run the firm: They know its strengths and weaknesses, its culture, its governance intricacies, its difficult personalities and its territorial wars.

They will also have an appreciation of cyber risk – at their level – because it's constantly in the news and many would have been exposed to it, in their current job or elsewhere.

This appreciation will be rooted in the broader risk context the firm is facing, and in its general risk management practices. This is well illustrated by this great piece from McKinsey. (McKinsey, Actions the best CEOs are taking in 2023, 2023)

That's the context CISOs need to grasp and in which their approach needs to be rooted, before jumping to ready-made technical assumptions and asking for millions.

If they achieve it and connect their demands – and their delivery – to the expectations of senior executives, they stand a chance of entering a virtuous circle where trust breeds success and success breeds trust and start to break up the endemic spiral of failure that has been plaguing cybersecurity practices for the last two decades.

Keep Appointing Pure Technologists in CISO Roles, and You'll Never Win

The WannaCry ransomware attack that affected so many large firms in May 2017 led to a number of animated discussions among InfoSec communities. The corrective patch (fixing the vulnerability targeted by the malware) was out in March for supported systems, and many firms were badly hit because of their reliance on the unsupported Windows XP (which reached the end of life in 2014).

The timely deployment of security patches has been regarded as a good fundamental security practice since the Code Red, Slammer, and Blaster virus outbreaks over ten years ago, so how can it be that so many large firms are still struggling with this today?

It cannot be just a matter of security investment. Many of the firms reportedly affected by the WannaCry outbreak would have had fully functioning security practices all that time and would have been spending millions every year on security products.

It has to be a plain matter of adverse prioritisation of security issues by IT and business leaders – which brings under the spotlight the role and profile of the CISO in those firms. Surely, it would have been the CISO's job to ensure that those matters remain on the agenda of the right leaders: to communicate their urgency, to drive remedial programmes, and to keep hammering at it until it gets fixed.

What is the security community doing wrong if it is collectively unable to address a technical issue such as the timely deployment of security patches over a period spanning more than a decade?

One reason often put forward by security technologists refers to a language disconnect between the CISO and the business. Somehow, CISOs are not being heard by business leaders and need to learn to 'speak the language of the business.' Such an assertion in itself raises concerns about the actual profile of the CISO if there are question marks over their ability to rise above mere technological arguments and present them in a language a non-specialist would understand.

Of course, many CISOs are technologists by background, and frankly, security has rarely been seen as a pathway to the top in IT circles, so very often, the CISO is either in that job because of a personal interest in the technical aspects of the topic ... or because there was little else for them to do.

To break the spiral that has led to the past 'lost decade' on cybersecurity matters, you urgently need to inject talent into the security industry. It is primarily managerial excellence that is missing, and it will have to be attracted by rewarding the right skills at the right level. It is also a matter of cultural transformation for many firms because it is about changing the value scale on which security is being judged.

To attract the best leaders, security (i.e., the protection of a firm's assets) has to be seen from the board down as something fundamental that the firm values and rewards, not something you can compromise on to maximise profits or imposed upon you arbitrarily by regulators.

And if you want your CISO to 'talk the language of the business,' you could start by appointing someone from the business – or at least an IT leader who is not a mere technology hobbyist and has a true transversal view of your business.

A lot of this is about context. If you present the patch deployment issue as an IT issue, you will be heard by your business in an IT context and prioritised against other IT topics. If you present it as a matter of fundamental protection against real and active threats, you will be engaging at a different level. But as a CISO, you will need the right voice, the right gravitas, and the right profile in the firm to be heard.

This is not only a rational argument. You'll have to use every fact you can find and always focus your communication with other business leaders on those facts and the reality of the threats. You'll have to pick your battles and strike at the right time to convince the right people. You'll have to break the 'bias of imaginability' (theorised by Kahneman), and it will take time. This is a very serious management role that requires a truly senior profile, a considerable amount of experience, and a willingness to stay on for the right course – and that could be considerably more than a mere couple of years.

Keep appointing pure technologists in CISO roles, and you'll never win. The level of information protection the firm needs to function is not a mere technology matter, contrary to what many tech vendors would like you to believe. It has a profound cultural dimension that is at the heart of the relationship between the firm and its employees. You naturally protect what you care about. If your CISO embodies that relation, everything they do will carry that weight, and you'll move forward.

Security Culture and Governance Eat Tech for Breakfast

Looking back at what happened at ground level throughout the COVID crisis, it is clear that the focus has been entirely on operational matters: from moving into remote working at scale for the services industry, to keeping supply chains working for the manufacturing sector, or to many retail firms having to reinvent themselves as digital businesses literally within weeks. It has all been about keeping the lights on, understandably.

Tech and cybersecurity have been – and still are – at the heart of all this, and it is hard not to see those sectors coming out as winners once the dust has finally settled over the pandemic, its economic aftermath, and the changes in the geopolitical context that followed.

But for now, the focus still appears to remain entirely tactical; many firms cannot really see beyond the short term, and it is likely to remain the case for the best part of the years ahead. This is hard to criticise as a business approach, given the scale and depth of the ongoing crisis; but in many firms, when it comes to cybersecurity, it is simply perpetuating and aggravating an endemic tendency – which, over the past ten years, has kept CISOs trapped in endless firefighting, prevented them from developing in terms of leadership and management skills, and not brought forward the necessary maturity changes around security in terms of governance, organisation, and culture.

This will be a serious problem in many firms that would have been locked for years in slow-moving and expensive security programmes, and they now need to transform their security practices at pace as cybersecurity has become a pillar of their 'new normal.'

It is an illusion to think that all the tactical and operational focus that has been prevailing around cybersecurity since the start of the pandemic is transformative. It may be counterintuitive, but moving past this operational obsession with cybersecurity is key, as we look ahead, to unlock long-term transformational dynamics.

The idea that the consistent protection of the business from cyber threats can result entirely and purely from the implementation of technical tools – or ad hoc pen tests, for that matter – is fundamentally flawed in the absence of a coherent overarching vision.

Tactical knee-jerk reactions simply add layer upon layer of technical legacy. Over time, the subpar delivery of poorly selected tools breeds distrust with senior management, who can't help but see that breaches continue to happen in spite of the millions spent. The inefficient reverse-engineering of security processes around the capabilities of the tools leads to escalating operational costs, staff shortages, and apparent skill gaps. CISOs feel alienated and leave. All this builds a narrative in which security becomes a cost and a problem, and over time, nobody wins.

Throwing money at the problem – for the industries where that was still an option in the midst of the current crisis – is not the answer for firms where security maturity has stagnated as a result of decades of underinvestment and adverse prioritisation by the business.

More than ever, now is the time to think in terms of people first, then process, then technology, if the objective is to build a lasting transformational dynamic around cybersecurity.

It is a vision that has to come from the top and be relayed across all the silos of the enterprise.

Cybersecurity cannot be seen as the responsibility of the CIO or the CISO. It needs to be visible and credible as part of a coherent business purpose, communicated coherently to the staff by senior management and relayed – and enforced – by a proper governance framework.

It is the embedding of security values in corporate culture and corporate governance that should drive the transformative efforts around cybersecurity and lead ultimately to effective cyber resilience.

This is certainly harder to put in place than buying more tech or doing one more pen test, but it is the key to long-term, transformative success around cybersecurity – in particular as younger generations become more and more sensitive to the clarity of purpose and positive business values.

2

The Problem with 'Technology-First' Approaches

. . . .

Cybersecurity Transformation Is Rooted in Governance and Culture, Not Technology

Compliance- and audit-oriented 'tick-in-the-box' practices are still underpinning many InfoSec strategies.

Huge sums of money are being spent on supposedly 'one-size-fits-all,' reactive solutions to one-off threats. However, such a firefighter mentality is at odds with the holistic, preventive protection that an efficient twenty-first-century InfoSec strategy requires.

Cyber threats have become increasingly salient for most organisations, with potentially fatal consequences in terms of operations, finance, and reputation. The board must realise the growing ubiquity of such threats – and the hard, cold fact that cyberattacks are no longer a matter of if but a matter of when.

This is not just a technology problem.

Your organisation forms the most efficient shield against potential threats, and as such, a transition towards an effective InfoSec governance is the only way ahead. A clear, simple, and consistent security mindset must be embedded at every level of the organisation. For many large organisations, this is no longer a matter of awareness development, but a profound matter of cultural change.

Rome was not built in a day, and neither will be a lasting InfoSec culture. As with any organisational change, it will always be a medium- to long-term journey.

For most of the Roman Empire's glory, the protection of the City of Rome was deemed a secondary issue, which could be addressed on an ad hoc basis with interventions by the Roman Army. It took the Romans more than three hundred years, and the pressure of a growing crisis due to barbarian threats, to finally decide to build the Aurelian Walls as a consistent and lasting security strategy for their city. They took four years to build, but they protected the city for almost two centuries.

As cybersecurity transformation experts, we feel a lesson can be drawn from history. Most organisations' current approach to InfoSec is, in many regards, very similar to that of overconfident Roman emperors: short-term-oriented, overly expensive, and inefficient in the face of growing threats. Good practices have existed for decades and will go a long way to protect against those threats, but they need to be in place.

In that respect, for many large organisations, driving cybersecurity change starts by looking back and removing the roadblocks that have prevented action in the past. All those (underinvestment, adverse prioritisation, complacency) do challenge governance and cultural practices up to board level. Addressing them is a complex management exercise – and definitely not an IT matter.

The Misleading Message of the Technology Industry

There is an incredible amount of material online and on social media around cybersecurity. But the vast majority of it is either sponsored by technology vendors or directly associated with them. They range from start-ups or specialised software houses (large and small) all the way up to industry heavyweights. They sponsor industry events, conferences, and publications of all sorts, including the specialised supplements of many broadsheets and magazines. They produce white papers, reports, surveys, and the like in numbers sufficient to fill several bookcases every year.

Broadly speaking, those reports have been saying the same thing for the past few years:

- Cyber threats are evolving faster than people can react.

- Investments in cybersecurity are insufficient to keep up.

- Maturity stays at low levels in large corporations and across the public sector.

- It must now become a 'board-level priority' for things to change.

Some of those aspects match what we observe in the field every day, but the overall message coming from technology vendors is simplistic and has two major flaws:

1. It tricks large corporations and the general public into believing that cybersecurity is something new.

This is not the case. Cyber threats have not appeared overnight. In fact, they have been evolving for the best part of the last fifteen years, and therefore there is a vast body of good practice that will go a long way to protect any business.

Those good practices have to be in place but often are not. Cutting corners around those on grounds of costs or convenience simply creates opportunities that cyber threats can target. And indeed, many recent breaches seem to relate to the absence of security controls that have been regarded as good practice for years and should have been in place. The sad reality is that, in spite of decades of spending in the information security space, many large organisations are still struggling today with problems going back to an era where security measures were seen as a necessary evil imposed by regulations – at odds with functionality and preventing innovation and agility.

2. It perpetuates the false idea that the problem is technical in nature.

In fact, it is increasingly becoming a matter of mindset, culture, and governance.

Many problems are rooted in decades of neglect, badly targeted investments, adverse prioritisation, or complacency.

And there can be no miracle solution – technical or otherwise – in such situations. Avoiding cybersecurity breaches, or dealing with them, requires coherent action over time across the whole organisation.

Only by identifying and removing the roadblocks that have prevented progress in the past can large organisations establish a genuine and lasting transformation dynamic. This is often a complex change process that could take years and require a relentless drive to succeed. It is not about deploying yet another piece of security software.

Of course, technology can and does enable some aspects of the cybersecurity transformation, but it needs to be rooted in a transformative vision that puts people and process first. And it needs to be embedded within a target operating model that allocates clear roles and responsibilities across the whole enterprise, not just the IT department.

These messages are rarely heard in the media, which is often dominated by the short-term agenda of tech vendors. Even when they do get mentioned, they are often lost in the midst of a vast amount of technology noise and are hardly audible or credible.

True independence is a rare commodity in the cybersecurity world, but it is essential for large organisations to navigate those waters and develop a genuinely protective practice, instead of simply listening to the latest technology buzz.

Why Are We Still Facing So Many Security Products and Vendors?

For me, this is a clear symptom of the unhealthy relationship between cybersecurity and large firms:

Each year, as we reach some high point in the conference season, one has to reflect once more on the staggering number of products and vendors active across the cybersecurity space.

Once again, they will invariably line up in their hundreds at each event. Of course, not all of them are making money; many are still burning the cash of their generous VCs. But the fact that such a crowded market still attracts large amounts of investment is still, in itself, bewildering.

In addition, many of those products still aim to address security requirements that are as old as good security practices themselves (e.g., across segments such as incident and event management or identity and access management).

To see those segments so fragmented across so many players after fifteen or twenty years of evolution is not a sign of a healthy marketplace. They should have been consolidated years ago, and each should have been dominated by a few players, in addition to the usual big names, all bound by healthy competition.

The fact that it's not the case simply tells us that the buyers are not serious. They do not buy those products because they address a real business need. They only buy those products to put ticks in compliance boxes; close down some audit points; support somebody's pet project; or, very often, in reactive mode and under pressure to show responsiveness after an incident – without any attempt or time to analyse the market, compare offerings, and structure a defensive strategy.

Even if the 'tick-in-the-box' market is huge (and GDPR has just made it bigger), in the long term, nobody wins at that game. Product development ends up being driven by regressive compliance-led dynamics instead of positive dynamics aimed at countering ever-evolving threats. Poorly protected buyers get breached, and the industry at large stagnates.

In many large organisations, the situation has reached astounding levels. Amongst others, the Cisco CISO benchmark study was highlighting already in 2019 that 37 percent of respondents had more than ten security vendors to manage (3 percent had more than fifty!) (Cisco, 2019).

'Best of breed' may be an interesting concept in the security space, but as we pointed out above, it is rarely the real reason behind product proliferation, and in practice, it presents operational teams with considerable challenges:

- How to orchestrate an efficient incident response when the data you need is scattered across so many platforms
- How to build an effective and meaningful reporting capability

The situation is often compounded by the fact that many security tools only end up being partially deployed or simply covering a fraction of the estate – functionally or geographically.

Firms that find themselves in that mess must stop buying more tech, look back at their genuine security requirements in relation to the threats they face, and start building a consolidation strategy.

They should also look beyond the products' marketplace and consider the ever-growing service offerings in that space. MSSPs have been active for over fifteen years, but the cloud has also facilitated the emergence of a number of new players in recent years.

Consolidation and integration become key factors as the 'when, not if' paradigm around cyberattacks takes centre stage with senior executives and their focus shifts away from risk and compliance towards execution and delivery.

All those who have been riding the compliance wave should bear that in mind.

Knee-Jerk Reactions to Data Breaches Are Damaging the Case for Cybersecurity

Cybersecurity transformation is not about implementing yet another technology product.

Anybody who has spent a few years in InfoSec management has seen this happen. Following an internal near-miss or some high-profile security incident widely publicised in the media, the same senior executives – who previously wouldn't bat an eyelid over information security issues – suddenly start panicking. Priorities shift. Immediate solutions are demanded. Money appears out of nowhere by the millions. Tech vendors are lined up. Some product is purchased that will allegedly fix everything. A box is checked, then normality returns.

Over the short term, only the tech vendors win – shamelessly – in these scenarios.

The CISO, if there is one, loses ground in most cases – unless they're just a technology hobbyist and they get another pet project to play with. Otherwise, they are likely to see their priorities turned upside down by the arrival of the new initiative and their ongoing projects being deprioritised in its favour.

This could be hugely demoralising for the CISO and their team, who might have worked hard for years to get some projects started that are now put on hold while other topics, which were repeatedly proposed and refused, are now being pushed forward by the same executives who previously turned them down:

- It damages the credibility of senior management with the cybersecurity professionals.

- It makes life more difficult for the cybersecurity team in their day-to-day interaction with IT teams, as they are seen as constantly 'moving the goalpost.'

- It perpetuates the wrong idea among IT communities that cybersecurity is just a topic you throw money at from time to time.

- In the long run, it alienates talent away from cybersecurity roles.

Cybersecurity products – broadly speaking – tend to do what they are supposed to do, so the chosen technology solution may provide a degree of protection to the organisation, but only if it gets implemented properly. And that's often the key issue. The product would have been selected in an emergency to plug a technical hole, not necessarily on the basis of the most thorough requirements analysis or market research.

- It may not be suited to the company's environment (e.g., deploying internal security products while key IT assets are in the cloud, or deploying internet security products if your internet footprint is limited).

- There may be competing products or solutions already in place internally that could have been leveraged (e.g., in different geographies or business lines). Ignoring these alienates and demotivates part of the organisation and may deprive the initiative of invaluable field experience around the topic.

- There may be considerable process issues when trying to embed the new product into legacy practices (e.g., around identity and access management or patch management), potentially leading to escalating costs, deployment limitations, or project failure.

Overall, the knee-jerk decision may end up being an expensive 'tick-in-a-box' exercise that achieves very little in practice.

Even for tech vendors, the situation may not be ideal in the longer term. As deployment fails or stalls due to technical issues, and value is limited by the lack of compatibility with people and processes, vendors may face dwindling revenue from subscriptions or cancellations of maintenance charges, which may damage the business models or investors' confidence.

Senior executives need to understand the dynamics they create where they demand instant solutions to problems that are, in reality, rooted in decades of underinvestment, adverse prioritisation, or complacency. And the CIO and the CISO need to have the management gravitas and the backbone to stand up to the board – with the right arguments – on those matters.

The harsh reality is that there can be no miracle solution – technical or otherwise – to such problems.

There may be a need for short-term tactical initiatives to demonstrate to the board, shareholders, or regulators that a new dynamic is being created around cybersecurity, but those have to be calibrated to the real maturity of the organisation around those matters and the genuine threats it faces. As importantly, it must be accompanied by a thorough examination of the cultural roadblocks that have prevented progress in the past.

A genuine and lasting transformation around cybersecurity can only come from the removal of those and from the definition of a long-term, transformative vision for the function – a vision that must come from the top and resonate across the whole organisation, not just IT.

There Are Just Too Many Security Tools and Products

Most large organisations are suffering from a security solutions proliferation problem which complexifies their operations beyond what is currently manageable and requires levels of resources to scale up which are simply not available in the current skills market.

This is the result of decades of organic development of cybersecurity practices, without any significant architectural effort over the mid to long-term, compounded by panic buying in response to incidents and knee-jerk reactions to put ticks in boxes after audit or regulatory observations.

This purely reactive approach to cybersecurity has had a perverse effect on the marketplace, because, in fact, it is often coupled with poor procurement and selection practices.

CISOs, under pressure on a number of fronts, often follow the path of least resistance: They go back to tools and vendors they know, or solutions they have used elsewhere.

Procurement practices, also under pressure in large firms, tend to focus on large contract values and major suppliers, allowing security vendors to stay off their radar.

Because many of those tools are purchased in urgency, from known vendors, without procurement scrutiny, there is often little pressure on prices.

Vendors can appear to be successful – to their investors – with relatively limited features because their tools are simply purchased as point-solutions and are rarely evaluated thoroughly against their competitors.

This is the engine that has led to the proliferation of tools and solutions we can see today, and has allowed countless cyber vendors to parade every year at all the tech shows.

But in addition, many of those tools are rarely deployed or used extensively, either because priorities shift, budget runs out, the CISO leaves, or the project stops after addressing low-hanging fruits.

So not only can vendors appear to be successful with relatively limited features, but they can also appear to be successful if those features don't work very well, because they are rarely tested at scale.

This is why CISOs often need more tools to fix what the existing tools cannot do, compounding the 'solutions' proliferation problem large firms are facing, and leading to the over-engineering of security operational processes, excessively manual investigation and response procedures, and SOC analysts burnouts.

Meanwhile breaches keep happening and business leaders wonder whether the millions invested in cyber over the years were really worthwhile.

CISOs and the security industry at large need to reflect on the resulting situation.

The skills gap is real across the industry and the piling-up of tools is just aggravating it.

The focus needs to shift from point-solutions towards a structured approach to security automation and the decluttering of the toolkit landscape.

'Good Security Governance' Is Not a Piece of Useless Consultant Jargon

Of course, cybersecurity has an intrinsic technical dimension and the protection of any firm against cyber threats will require the application of technical countermeasures at a number of levels. But there are countless tech vendors and service providers out there trying to sell their products as the silver bullet that will protect you from anything. And countless small firms are still holding simplistic views on cyber threats:

'We're fine, all our data is in the cloud.'

For any organisation above a certain size, effective and efficient protection can only result from the layered application of protective measures at the people, process, and technology levels – in that order.

It has to start with people, and that doesn't mean rolling out a security awareness programme. Middle management has always had the tendency to jump straight into the solution space at the back of a simplistic analysis of the problem, but at the heart of the 'people' aspects of any security strategy lie issues of corporate culture and corporate governance.

'Good security governance' is not a piece of useless consultant jargon. It is an essential protective layer for any organisation.

It ensures a visible endorsement of security values from the top down; it brings clarity around security roles, responsibilities, and accountabilities across the whole organisation; and more importantly, it is the cornerstone that 'gets things done' around security through an effective and efficient layer of reporting.

Only the actual execution of security measures (i.e., the actual deployment of security processes and the technology required to support them) will protect the business. And that's where many organisations, large and small, have failed over the past decades in spite of colossal investments in cybersecurity. Security projects get deprioritised halfway through or focus only on non-existent low-hanging fruits. Over time, people get demotivated and leave, nothing gets finished, and half-baked 'solutions' proliferate.

Let's get this straight. This is plain governance failure, and it has been plaguing organisations, large and small, around security for the best part of the last two decades.

To avoid those mistakes, break that spiral, and target the management and governance roadblocks that have prevented progress in the past, most organisations need to act at three levels:

First, get a good understanding of your security maturity posture to start with, and set realistic time frames around change. Change takes 'the time it takes,' and there may be no quick wins.

Then, be objective about the skills and resources that you have to deliver change, and set realistic improvement goals. Jumping straight at ineffective 'virtual CISO' solutions in the hope of making the problem disappear will not help if nobody is there to execute them.

Finally, stay focused. Security transformation often involves a change in mindset that needs stability to develop and takes time to set in. Changing directions or priorities every time something happens in the business or elsewhere will simply kill any transformational momentum around security.

The Problem with Cybersecurity ROI

If the reporting line of the CISO is the oldest ongoing topic of discussion among cybersecurity communities, security ROI is probably the second oldest.

CISOs being asked those questions should look beyond the topic itself and face the underlying issues it might be hiding.

In reality, it hides several endemic problems that have been plaguing the security industry for the last two decades.

First of all, it downgrades cybersecurity to a mere matter of investments – which would have to be justified – implying that lack of funding and lack of resources are at the heart of low security maturity levels and the cyberattacks epidemic we have been seeing for the last ten years.

In fact, problems have largely been elsewhere. Large organisations have committed billions collectively to cybersecurity over the period; it's governance and cultural issues that have led to adverse prioritisation and execution failure.

While it may be the case that some organisations have not invested enough in relation to the threats they face, the security ROI discussions are often the sign of arbitrary programmes of work driven bottom-up by a CISO, either replicating recipes applied elsewhere or listening to the sirens of some tech vendors, when not simply pushing their own pet projects.

Cybersecurity did not appear overnight with the COVID pandemic. Any large organisation will have a history and a legacy of some sort in that space spanning two decades.

Understanding the investments made in the past – what has worked, what hasn't (and the reasons why) – and showing decision makers that lessons are being learnt around past execution failures would be more important to building trust than a financial ROI calculation that will be invariably plagued by disputable assumptions and estimates, leaving it vulnerable to internal politics and horse-trading around numbers.

Because very often, trust (or the lack of it) is at the heart of the context here, in particular when the ROI question comes top-down onto the CISO. Many CISOs take it as a normal business question and a natural justification to give, while in fact, it tends to mean, 'I am not sure I understand what you are trying to do and why you want to spend so much.'

It is a rare concern at the top these days, in the face of non-stop cyberattacks and data breaches. Boards are often more concerned with demonstrating they are spending enough on cyber.

So the persistence of the cybersecurity ROI debates is to be seen in my view as a symptom of the distrust, a lack of positive engagement between the CISO and senior stakeholders, and a defence mechanism on their part.

Any large organisation would have spent millions or tens of millions – if not more – on cybersecurity over the past decades. You cannot blame senior executives for being suspicious when they see in front of them yet another investment plan in that space.

Instead of jumping straight into a financial ROI debate where they are likely to lose credit, CISOs who want to drive large-scale, transformative programmes around cybersecurity should focus first on building trust with senior stakeholders and solid communication channels with all of them, working across silos towards business units, geographies, and support functions (such as legal, HR, or procurement, as well as IT and their suppliers).

Even if they are working towards the delivery of a long-term, large-scale road map, they should split it into cheaper, more manageable chunks to demonstrate their execution capabilities with simple and achievable tasks, addressing business expectations before getting to meatier (and more expensive) matters.

By then, their own clarity of vision and their ability to execute should carry them sufficiently to avoid arbitrary – and often useless – discussions around ROI.

That's the key element to remember around cybersecurity ROI discussions: They shouldn't be happening at all in the current context, given the non-stop avalanche of cyberattacks we are seeing worldwide.

Time to Bring the Cybersecurity Technical Debt under Control

For the past two decades, most large organisations have kept addressing cybersecurity as a purely technical problem. And let's face it: Many are failing to protect themselves, not just because the threats morph constantly and faster than they can adapt, but primarily because of endemic execution problems around the deployment of technical solutions and the disconnect between primarily short-termist business cycles and the longer time frames required to develop cybersecurity maturity levels in large firms.

In short, cybersecurity strategies are invariably architected around technical projects and tools, but deployment rarely goes beyond alleged quick wins. This is because business priorities shift constantly and rarely look over the medium to long term – as would be required in many firms to deliver real and lasting change around cybersecurity.

CISOs leave after a few years out of frustration over slow progress (and for more money), and the technical debt keeps piling up – all tendencies that have been greatly aggravated by the COVID pandemic.

After two decades of playing that game, some cybersecurity practices are now operating around up to twenty or thirty different tools in large organisations.

Nothing is ever joined up because it is simply the result of decades of organic short-termism; 'strategic' plans that were never strategic or never rolled out; and knee-jerk reactions in response to incidents, audit observations, or panic buying ahead of regulatory inspections.

It results in complex security operational processes: poorly integrated, excessively manual, repetitive and boring for the analysts in charge of delivering them, and tremendously expensive to scale up – if you can find the skills, that is.

Because most industry sectors have woken up to the criticalness of cybersecurity following the avalanche of cyberattacks we have been seeing over the past decade, they are now competing for a resource pool that has not grown sufficiently over the period.

People asking themselves why it has not grown sufficiently need to look beyond educational and training issues. It is not only the talent acquisition rate that is too low across the cybersecurity industry. It is also the retention rate, and that is essentially linked to those dysfunctional operational processes and the 'boring' entry-level jobs of many analysts, who undoubtedly didn't get into cybersecurity to end up cutting and pasting data into Excel sheets or producing useless reports simply designed to put ticks in compliance boxes. At the first available opportunity, they leave to do something more exciting, and they don't come back.

At the heart of this, conveniently fuelled by the tech industry, lies the excessive focus on tech products to solve cybersecurity challenges, the reverse engineering of processes around the capabilities of tools, and the colossal accumulation of technical debt in that space over the past two decades, which is the result of execution failures and lack of priority focus by business leaders.

Senior executives who want to break out of that spiral need to stop buying more tech for the sake of it and start focusing on decluttering their cybersecurity landscape.

'For every one new solution, remove two legacy solutions,' suggested Greg Day (at the time, VP and CSO, EMEA, Palo Alto Networks) in an interview with InfoSecurity Magazine (InfoSecurity, 2021).

It sounds like a good start. But to achieve that, cybersecurity leaders will have to look back at the structure of their operational processes and streamline those.

They will also have to look differently at automation and focus it on improving analysts' efficiency, allowing them to dedicate more time to the challenging tasks for which they have been trained and hired.

Ultimately, cybersecurity leaders will have to go back where all this should have started: people, process, then technology – technology not for technology's sake but in support of security processes that are designed to protect the firm and its people from the cyber threats they face.

It is more difficult to execute and sell internally than buying the next shiny tool to put a tick in some compliance box, but stopping the creation of technical debt and bringing the existing one under control have become vital to the future of the cybersecurity industry.

The Cybersecurity Parallel Universe

It's about time we go back to basics with most of our cybersecurity commentaries.

Sometimes I wonder if some cybersecurity experts, journalists or tech vendors live in a parallel universe.

They would have you believe that quantum computing and its impact on current cryptography, or cybersecurity in the metaverse should be on the agenda of any CISO, and that zero-trust (or whatever tech they sell) will solve all the problems of the industry; that all problems come invariably from a lack of 'user awareness', and that all solutions can only involve buying new technical tools (the ones the sell or represent, obviously).

Meanwhile, CISOs and other field practitioners struggle with a different reality:

- HR departments unwilling to accept a role in joiners and leavers processes, or pretending they do not handle sensitive personal data;
- IT departments still failing at patch deployment or at building a unified CMDB across their estate in spite of 15 years of investments in those areas;
- Legal departments treating compliance around data privacy as a matter of regulatory risk.

It's about time we go back to basics with most of our cybersecurity commentaries and refocus attention on a few key points:

Ownership of the matter is key: This is no longer about 'wheeling in' the CISO in front of the board every year, or every time something happens somewhere. This is about the board owning cybersecurity as a board-level topic, and handling it as a board-level topic, not as something you delegate down because it is 'too technical'.

Cybersecurity is not the responsibility of the security team. Key stakeholders have to be identified across business units, geographies and support functions and made accountable for the adequate handling of cybersecurity matters at their level, as part of a structured operating model, under the supervision of a board member.

This is no longer just a matter of throwing money at the problems: Buying more tech and focusing only on operational matters is not likely to help with those, where cybersecurity maturity has remained low over the past decades in spite of all investments in that space.

Two aspects are key to acknowledge:

- Cybersecurity didn't appear with the COVID crisis or the ransomware epidemic, and doing the basics right still provide a good degree of protection against most threats and a good degree of compliance against most regulations.

- Large organisations have been spending billions collectively with security vendors and consultants over the years, and without identifying where the roadblocks have been in the past which have prevented those investments to come to fruition, nothing will change.

Looking at the topic through that prism will invariably take senior executives towards governance and cultural matters: Endemic short-termism leading to adverse prioritisation of security matters, incapacity of the organisation to look beyond alleged 'quick wins', endless merry-go-round of cybersecurity leaders...

Real and lasting change takes time and relentless drive, and many large organisations struggle with long-term focus, in particular with complex and transversal matters such as cybersecurity.

Nevertheless, this spiral of failure can only be broken top-down, by pragmatic senior executives willing to confront the field reality of their problems in that space, without listening to the hype and the sirens of the tech world.

Cybersecurity problems can only be resolved in the real world, not in the parallel universe of tech vendors.

3

The Consequences on Operational Security and Talent Retention

A Real life Take on the Cybersecurity Skills Gap

You don't have to go far these days to find security professionals complaining about skills shortages and countless media outlets relaying their views. But there are at least two sides to this argument, and the situation requires a more balanced approach.

There is no doubt – first of all – that the cybersecurity industry still has an image problem. It often carries a dated tech-heavy narrative and ends up being perceived as an obscure and complex technical niche, something reserved for nerds and geeks. When the excellent ladies of the CEFCYS in Paris published their first guide to the cybersecurity professions earlier this year, they titled it 'I Don't Wear a Hoodie, Yet I Work in Cybersecurity.' (CEFCYS, 2020)

In fact, the security industry has never managed to make itself attractive, and in turn, the lack of awareness around the diversity of security roles breeds a lack of relevant training courses and educational opportunities.

The absence of clear security career paths is also a real problem at all levels when it comes to attracting new talent. What do you do once you have been a security analyst in a SOC for a few years (or a CISO for that matter)? You should not have to be condemned to hopping across similar roles all the time, but credible alternative role models are cruelly missing. How many CISOs have actually become CIO, COO, or CRO?

However, this is rarely what people refer to when they talk about the 'cybersecurity skills gap.' They often refer to problems in staffing large security initiatives or security operation centres, and here the so-called skills gap is often a fig leaf hiding different problems.

Many security leaders, in particular in large organisations, are stuck with legacy operational processes around identity management, security monitoring, incident handling, or threat intelligence – which are mostly manual, labour-intensive, repetitive, and built around countless tools.

Attracting – and retaining – young professionals in such jobs can indeed be hard. It is even harder in the absence of clear career paths and role models, as we highlighted above.

Also, many large organisations, faced with large-scale maturity problems and urgent security transformation challenges, are trying – unrealistically – to fix all their problems at the same time. But building a monstrous programme of work requiring in theory tens of additional FTEs, and ignoring all dependencies between tasks and cultural aspects, is not how you change things. You would struggle to staff it in any specialised industry – and to deliver it. This is just bad planning, and it is fuelled by the tech industry and large consultancies.

So does all this reflect a real shortage of skills – or a shortage of appetite from the leadership to tackle the reengineering of legacy security processes to make them attractive and better suited to the expectations of a younger workforce? Or is the alleged shortage of skills simply an excuse to hide poor management and the greed of the security ecosystem?

Ultimately, all those aspects are just the different sides of the same problem. To attract more raw talent into the security industry (at all levels, security management included), you have to make it more attractive in a credible and meaningful way – at all levels.

To help with that at analyst level, the leadership should focus on decluttering the cybersecurity estates and automating processes intelligently to allow a smaller number of analysts to work more efficiently, creating a more stimulating – and less boring – environment for them.

At the middle and senior level, the focus should be on building role models and career paths, showcasing real, meaningful, and credible bridges across cybersecurity roles and other roles – at least across the broader GRC spectrum but ideally across the entire management spectrum. Looking beyond tech is absolutely key in that space. There is no reason why a CISO would not come from a business role.

Professional bodies and industry bodies have a role to play here to rebuild that narrative and help the security industry become more attractive and move forward.

The Constant Confusion between Tool and Process

There are real issues in the security operations space but buying more tools won't help.

The 2021 survey from TrendMicro paints a slightly frightening picture of the state of security operations in large firms (TrendMicro, 2021): twenty-nine monitoring solutions in place on average and analysts stressed out, unhappy, drowning in alerts, and spending 27 percent of their time dealing with false positives and ending up ignoring or turning off alerts.

All these are to be taken with a reasonable dose of caution, coming from a tech vendor active in that space, but also matching anecdotal evidence we see in the field regularly.

As always, with those, the conclusion of the survey is that you need to buy more tools to solve all highlighted problems (those sold by the people who commissioned the survey, of course). Nobody in the cybersecurity tech industry seems to see the irony behind that type of report.

Still, they put in perspective some real issues in the security operations space.

The tool-proliferation problem is real and ancient, aggravated by the COVID crisis that has accentuated short-termist and tactical tendencies and engineered countless knee-jerk reactions around cybersecurity that have just created more technical debt in that space.

Security operational processes are intrinsically inefficient because they have been – almost always – reversely engineered around the capabilities of specific tools selected on a whim, under pressure, just to close down audit observations, or because the CISO 'used them elsewhere.'

Nothing is ever joined up because there was never any overarching vision beyond the immediate need (to close an audit point, to react to an incident). So operational tasks mushroom in all directions and become overlapping, repetitive, and poorly managed.

Meanwhile, analysts are burning out at the receiving end of those excessively manual processes and ending up leaving the cybersecurity industry to get out of boring jobs where they spend their day cutting and pasting data into Excel spreadsheets to produce useless reports designed to put ticks in compliance boxes ... The whole thing becomes attritive and simply alienates talent at all levels.

At the heart of the problem lies – conveniently put there by the tech industry – the constant confusion between tool and process.

Just to take a few examples, the acronyms DLP (data loss prevention) or IAM (identity and access management) by themselves do not refer to tools or sets of tools; they refer literally to the description of processes.

Any DLP implementation project, for example, must start with an identification of key stakeholders, the sensitive data to protect, the way it is currently exchanged, the way it is currently tagged or labelled (or not), the objectives and constraints of the stakeholders around the protection of the data, the internal or external threats susceptible to steal or leak the data, and finally leading to building up a way to engineer DLP (as a process) to make it work across the firm. (t should include process elements such as the handling of anomalies and alerts and the granting of temporary or permanent exceptions, themselves probably subject to some form of approval workflow (or the interfacing of the DLP process with pre-existing processes in that space).

It's only once you have gone through that phase of analysis and process design that you should start looking for tools to enable your DLP initiative to succeed.

Starting the other way round (i.e., starting with tool selection and defining the process around the capabilities of the selected tool) is bound to create friction with pre-existing practices and the expectations or capabilities of stakeholders, leading to poor deployment, poor acceptance, or both.

As CISOs, I am sure we have all done it under pressure at some stage of our careers (I know I have). But it remains a mistake – and probably one of the costliest for a CISO to make – because it creates distrust with stakeholders and, over time, with senior management, who can't help but see the escalating financial demands from CISOs in return for poor execution and continuing breaches.

The solution to the broader security operations problem lies in decluttering the cybersecurity estates, through reengineering and smart automation of operational processes.

I like the suggestion from Greg Day already quoted above:

'For every one new solution, remove two legacy solutions.' (InfoSecurity, 2021)

But once again, to achieve this, you have to start from the process end of your practice. The 'one new solution' you add has to be added from a perspective of process realignment and simplification, and the two you remove have to be removed from the same perspective. Do not forget that processes are enacted by people who are creatures of habit and have to be trained and led on the path of change, not just expected to go with the flow.

In all cases, process has to come first, then people, then technology. The cybersecurity industry – listening to the sirens of tech vendors – has been doing it the other way around for the best part of the last twenty years. Now the accumulated burden becomes too much to carry in the face of unrelenting threats.

Things need to change, but buying more tools won't help unless they truly have estate decluttering and smart process automation at their heart.

Cybersecurity Automation Is Key to Fight the Skills Gap

To start building solutions to the skills gap problem, it is key to look at it in all its dimensions.

The debate around the cybersecurity skills gap continues to ride fairly high on the security industry's agenda, but to start building solutions, it is key to look at the problem in all its dimensions.

The cybersecurity skills gap problem has its origins in three interlocking factors:

There is undoubtedly a growing demand for cyber skills, rooted in long-term trends towards the digitisation of many industries and the avalanche of cyberattacks we have seen over the past ten years, both aspects greatly amplified by the COVID crisis.

Many organisations – large and small – that had never had an InfoSec function before now have one or are building one. Many organisations that didn't know what a pen test was are now getting regularly tested. We need far more cybersecurity analysts, developers, testers, and managers than ever before, and education and training programmes are struggling to keep up with the growth of the demand and the diversity of the roles.

But you cannot end the analysis at this point and conclude that the solution lies entirely in attracting and training more people. Because the problem has at least two additional dimensions you also need to act on.

Many large organisations tend to respond to the growing cybersecurity emergency by scaling up legacy operational processes and with the perpetuation of a culture that believes that the solution to all cybersecurity problems is technical in nature and requires more tools. This is fuelled by countless tech vendors and large consultancies, but also by many CISOs being technologists by trade and by background and hopping from job to job, carrying with them the same technical recipes. This has led to a proliferation of tools – poorly integrated, often partially deployed or implemented – that simply embeds manual steps within security operational processes in many large firms and dramatically increases their demand for resources and skills.

This is also attritive in nature, in particular at analyst-level and many entry-level cybersecurity roles, because it results in jobs that are excessively repetitive and boring, with limited career development options. So attracting and training more people is key to fixing the cybersecurity skills gap, certainly in the long run. But if you can't keep them in the industry (because you give them boring jobs to do and no career path), this has the potential to become a self-perpetuating problem.

To break this cycle, and in parallel to increasing long-term efforts around training at all levels, the security industry must look at the medium to short term, accelerate on automation and tools integration, and focus on decluttering legacy tooling landscapes and operational processes to give fewer analysts more exciting jobs where they can develop more and bring more value.

It is certainly more difficult for CISOs than just hiring more people. But jumping straight at AI-driven solutions (which may be immature or overhyped) is not the answer either – only a continuation of the same tech-driven obsession that has led to the proliferation of security tools in the first place.

Now more than ever, the key to driving a successful decluttering and automation project around cybersecurity is keeping things simple and focusing on people and process first, then technology.

Empirical, Bottom-Up, and Organically Developed Cybersecurity Functions Need to Evolve

Every year, various surveys come out analysing the state of the CISO profession, their priorities and their pain points.

Collectively, they often paint a slightly uncomfortable picture: the picture of CISO roles and security practices still operating bottom-up, disconnected from the dynamics of the business. When asked which concerns most affect their ability to deliver against objectives, many mention the culture of their organisation (as if they were not part of it), the speed of business change (as if it were happening all around them but without them) or the level of board support (although in response to another question, they would generally say they would like to report to board level).

It would be fascinating to ask some of the questions to the direct bosses of the respondents in those surveys and compare results.

Of course, in such a context of alienation from the business, budgets are hard to get by for CISOs. Frustration builds up and leads to attrition. When asked why they left their last role, most mention not having sufficient resources to make their role a success (in their view, of course); or frustration with their organisation's approach to security. Some go as far as mentioning 'not seeing eye to eye with senior leadership' in some surveys ...

But another shocking fact is that most respondents don't seem to have a security operating model in place. This element alone puts the rest of the surveys into perspective.

In the absence of a structured framework to work against, most cybersecurity practices can only operate 'as they go along,' in project mode or in firefighting mode.

How can you justify budgets and attract or retain talent without a referential to work against and in the absence of a clear governance model, roles, responsibilities, and to a degree, clear career paths? And again, how can you claim you do not have enough staff in the absence of a target operating model, detailing tasks and the resources required to deliver those tasks? It can only be a finger-in-the-air exercise, the very kind any half-decent CFO would smell miles away.

This kind of empirical, bottom-up, and organically developed cybersecurity function does not work and needs to evolve. What is required is structure, business acumen, and top-down engagement.

The emphasis on security culture throughout the report is valuable and meaningful, but it cannot be the only axis of action for the CISO. Security awareness has always been a low-hanging fruit and an easy sell for CISOs when they cannot find other levers. You can't go very wrong by distributing mouse mats and leaflets, and it does not cost the world. But this is not what culture change is about, and there cannot be any culture change that does not come from the top down.

The culture of alienation many CISOs have developed is probably comfortable for some; there is always someone to blame ('the business') and another juicy job to move into afterwards. But it does not help organisations and society at large.

To break this spiral of failure, the profile of the CISO needs to evolve, and the board needs to take ownership.

This is no longer just about tech – if it ever was. This is about protecting the business against cyberattacks that have now become a matter of 'when, not if.' This is no longer something you can push down in the organisation.

If the board does not see the need – or does not feel qualified – to step in, nothing will ever change for good around cybersecurity because it has simply become too complex and too transversal. Bottom-up approaches will continue to pour cash down the drain, CISOs will continue to leave every other year out of frustration, and breaches will continue to happen.

If the board wants to set directions, they should drive, appoint someone they trust and can talk to (it does not have to be a technologist), and empower that person to build or rebuild cybersecurity practices across the firm, in the light of what the board wants and expects.

Cybersecurity Maturity Stagnates Because Many CISOs Are Structurally Prevented from Looking Beyond Day-to-Day Firefighting

Many CISOs struggle to look beyond day-to-day firefighting and get trapped in tactical games. It is one of the major factors preventing organisations from developing better levels of cybersecurity maturity.

In many firms, this goes beyond incidents and the natural need to address those. It is often compounded by three structural elements literally trapping the CISO in tactical games, forcing endemic short tenures and creating the conditions for a systemic spiral of failure around cybersecurity.

1. First, corporate short-termism, which is still prevalent in many organisations among senior executive communities:

'In the long term, we're all dead,' and anything that would not impact the next quarter's figures does not grab the interest for very long. Cybersecurity matters are being pushed towards those levels of management by non-stop media reports around data breaches and the potential level of GDPR fines. But when faced with multiyear, seven- or eight-digit transformative programmes of work around security that would genuinely force the firm to alter the way it works, those executives often revert to what they've been doing for decades around compliance: looking for quick wins and cheap boxes to tick so that they can 'show progress' while minimising spend and disruption.

The problem with cybersecurity is that organisations facing that type of problem are generally in need of a structural overhaul of their security practices, and 'quick wins' are often non-existent. Driving real and lasting change takes time. Simply 'fixing' illusory quick wins has never been the base of any transformation.

2. Second, plain old office politics between IT and security – which have always been a component of the life of many CISOs, irrespective of their reporting line (and this is undoubtedly worse where the CISO does not report to the CIO):

Technologists are trained and incentivised to deliver functionality, not controls, and many over the past decades have developed a culture that sees security measures as constraints instead of requirements.

Many CISOs are constantly bombarded by 'urgent' requests to define security measures coming from IT people who should know better but are just 'passing the buck.'

The CISOs often feel that they would fail by not responding, not realising that this is a game they cannot win and a form of political and emotional blackmail that must be avoided, especially outside large organisations where teams and resources tend to be smaller. The CISO and their team simply cannot be expected to be deep technical security experts on all technology streams and across all platforms, or to 'drop everything' at any time to help projects.

Of course, they can rely on external skills (budgets permitting), but fundamentally, roles, responsibilities, and demarcation lines should be clear and resources placed where they should be. The security of IT systems should be the responsibility of the respective IT teams. The security team should assist, validate, and control while retaining a degree of independence. This is the spirit of all organisational models developed over the past twenty years around IT security. It should be clear, and the CISO and their boss should have the backbone to enforce it.

3. Finally, in many cases, the greed of the tech industry, which is only aggravating the situation:

For each of those alleged 'quick wins' or 'urgent' issues to fix, there are countless vendors bidding to sell their stuff to put a tick in that box, irrespective of any bigger picture.

This is a pressure the CISO must resist. Over time, this accumulation of point solutions simply leads to a product-proliferation problem that makes everything more difficult for the CISO and their team. From incident management to compliance reporting, security operations become burdened by the need to collect data across multiple platforms, often in inconsistent formats. Resources requirements escalate, and it aggravates the perception that security is just a cost and a pain, instead of a necessary barrier against real and active threats.

The CISO and IT must build the discipline to work with a small number of security vendors and service providers around which they can structure effective and efficient security operations, properly segregated and proportionate to the threats the business is facing and the resources available to fight them.

Clarity of roles and responsibilities across security and IT and a clear approach (putting people and process first ahead of ready-made technology solutions) are the bases on which the CISO can avoid the tactical trap. It is also the only basis on which cybersecurity maturity can grow, across any organisation, large or small.

A Different Take on the Short Tenure of the CISO

Looking Beyond Stress, Burnout, and Scapegoating Theories: What Is Really Going On?

I think an element of reflexion is required on the impact the short tenure of CISOs is having on the security industry at large and the evolution of the cybersecurity maturity of large firms.

First of all, many firms that never had a CISO before have opened up new positions across the last decade, and demand is strong from industry sectors that were never real players in the security space.

When I started attending security conferences over twenty years ago, most of my peers were in finance, Big Pharma, or the energy sector – regulated industries or industries where security has always worked hand in hand with safety and where safety has always been a pillar of the culture of the sector.

Today most industry sectors have some form of security practice in place. Recruitment activity around CISO roles is significant and profitable for recruiters. There is a significant shortage of quality management profiles in that space; salaries are high and are on the rise.

To put it simply, good CISOs get headhunted – at least around me. Some offers are just 'too good to turn down,' and a number of them simply 'follow the money.' But for others, things are rarely as straightforward, and here I would go back to Dan's analysis.

The decision to change jobs is often rooted in a negative context, and the call from the recruiter is just the catalyst that starts the process.

Clearly, CISOs don't seem to be a very happy bunch, and their frustration appears to be rooted in some form of disconnect with their management.

That's understandable. Many CISO positions were created in response to rampant cyber threats across the last decade in industries that had never had such roles in place. They were created tactically with the operational objective of preventing breaches, by senior executives who didn't really understand the context and the transversal complexity involved in the cyber protection of large organisations.

It created situations where many CISOs struggled with limited resources and constant attacks and never managed to build a meaningful narrative with management beyond mere firefighting. They might have hopped from job to job, but they carried the problem with them, and over the past decade, many CISOs have not been able to develop the leadership and management skills that they would need to elevate the role to the next level.

In parallel, expectations from management have changed. In the face of constant breaches in the news, the penny has finally dropped in many boardrooms, and the 'when, not if' paradigm around cyberattacks has taken root. Many boards have reached the point where they are ready to make very significant transformative investments around cybersecurity, but in exchange, they would demand faultless execution and delivery from their CISO.

That's what is putting many CISOs under unbearable pressure. Over the past decade, they have been prevented, by constant firefighting, from developing the softer skills – the personal gravitas and political acumen – that are key to delivering complex initiatives in large firms.

To me, this is the context in which the short tenure of CISOs has to be seen. A survey by Nominet estimated it at twenty-six months in 2020 (ZDNet, 2020) (Nominet, 2020). Anecdotal evidence from my network seems to back this up. Having analysed the LinkedIn profile of fifteen of my contacts currently in CISO positions, I have reached the figure of thirty months, each having held three different CISO positions on average throughout their career.

It is time to start recognising the impact this CISO 'merry-go-round' has had on the security industry over the past decade and on the evolution of security maturity in large firms.

You achieve very little in large organisations in two to three years, certainly very little that could have a lasting transformative impact – if that's what's required. At best, you kick start some projects, but each CISO comes in with their own culture, priorities, and approach, and your successor may or may not follow in your footsteps.

Over time distrust sets in with senior management, who can't help but notice that breaches keep happening in spite of the investments made in that space. Security becomes a cost and a problem – an area that no ambitious executive, internally, would consider as a possible career step.

This distrust and the spiral of failure fuelled by CISOs' short tenures are at the heart of the problem here, and over the last decade, the situation has become self-perpetuating.

As we wrote back in 2018, 'Nothing will change until the profile of the CISO is raised and they start to see their role over the mid to long term.' (CorixPartners, 2018)

To break this spiral, the board needs to own cybersecurity as a genuine board-level agenda item, elevate the topic and the role, build it up as a genuine career elevator to inject raw talent (probably from business circles), and create the conditions for trust to rebuild around business security objectives driven from the top down, instead of operational security objectives driven from the bottom up.

It may lead to the emergence of CSO types of roles, returning historical CISO roles to their original technical purpose. Now more than ever, this is crucial to driving real change across organisations made entirely dependent on digital services by the COVID crisis and its economic and geopolitical aftermath.

Towards a New Profile for the CISO

A decade of firefighting has taken its toll on the CISO profession.

The role of the CISO is changing. If that was ever the case, it can no longer be seen just as a technical role.

In some industries, it is being challenged by the worldwide tightening of regulations around privacy and the emergence of DPOs and other related roles.

Everywhere, it is being challenged by the non-stop avalanche of cyberattacks and data breaches over the past decade, which have raised the visibility of cybersecurity to board level but at the same time have also prevented many CISOs from getting out of firefighting mode.

This is the crux of the matter.

Senior executives are increasingly endorsing a 'when, not if' paradigm around cyberattacks and are demanding fundamental change and action beyond day-to-day firefighting, often in exchange for very significant investments around security.

They are expecting the CISO to lead such programmes of work, but many CISOs have never been recruited or trained for such a challenge, under such level of scrutiny. Very often, it is about addressing problems rooted in a decade of lip service or underinvestment around security, and it involves a true transformation of many business practices across the firm.

You don't become a transformational leader overnight – in particular if your background, your skills, and your core interests are centred around the more technical aspects of cybersecurity. Nothing is wrong with that. While the focus was on firefighting cyberattacks all the time, those would have been valuable qualities, but as the focus shifts towards transformation and execution, the ability to influence across silos and understand the true nature of the business and the more transversal aspects of security becomes paramount. Those are rarely attributes of a native technologist, and they are not attributes you develop through the constant firefighting of technical problems.

So parallel to the 'lost decade' of cybersecurity and reflecting it, there is also a lost decade for the CISO profession. It is a lost decade during which many have hopped from job to job, collecting higher and higher salaries for their technical firefighting skills, but without encountering the terrain in which to develop true enterprise-level leadership and transformational skills.

As senior executives turn a page and we enter – possibly – an execution-dominated decade around cybersecurity, many CISOs are just not equipped to lead.

Let's say this one more time: Just throwing money at cybersecurity problems won't make them disappear overnight. Remediating issues rooted in a decade of adverse prioritisation by the business will cost money, but it will also require time and, in many cases, a relentless drive to change mindsets.

Who should do this, if the CISO can't?

There are broadly two types of options:

Organisational models may need to evolve to allow a broader CSO type of role to emerge in large firms – encompassing security at large, continuity, and privacy – with the CISO role retreating back to its technical roots. This would, by itself, attract a different calibre of individuals into each role, and such rebalancing of skills could be key to the success of large-scale cybersecurity transformation programmes.

Alternatively, the profile of the CISO needs to change to adjust to the imperatives of the 'when, not if' era. It becomes essential to start prioritising leadership skills over technical skills and distributing roles across a structured function instead of looking for 'unicorn' profiles. Nobody can be credible on all fronts all day long, from the board down and horizontally across all functions and geographies of the business. Those profiles don't exist, and pretending otherwise is just setting up the CISO to fail.

4

How to Break Out of It

When True Innovation Consists of Doing Now What You Should Have Done Ten Years Ago

Year after year, major surveys highlight low levels of cybersecurity maturity across large firms and, increasingly, an even more worrying situation among smaller firms.

Most of those surveys have another point in common. They are, in some form or another, organised or sponsored by heavyweights of the cybersecurity industry or large consultancy firms, who ultimately can be suspected of having an interest in accentuating negative traits in order to maximise their own sales.

But even if the results of those surveys have to be taken with great care for that reason, they do match an enormous amount of anecdotal evidence we come across in the field every day. Too many large firms – leaders in their field – are still struggling with fundamental basic principles of cybersecurity hygiene that have been regarded as good practice for ten to fifteen years and for which technical solutions and organisational processes have been in existence for as long:

- Monitoring of basic network security events
- Timely deployment of security patches on servers and desktops
- Timely removal of user accounts
- Periodic revalidation of access levels with business units

It cannot be suggested that solving those problems is easy in large firms, and to a large extent, the disappearance of the traditional business perimeter of the enterprise and the digital transformation of supply and value chains have made things even more complex.

But those good practices have been relentlessly pushed forward by auditors and regulators, as well as InfoSec professionals, for the best part of the last ten to fifteen years. Very large amounts of money have been spent with tech vendors on alleged solutions in those areas, so undoubtedly, it is concerning that so little progress seems to have been made by so many firms in those domains over such a long period.

The most common root cause is a constant short-termist approach by senior management, focused solely on alleged 'quick wins,' or illusory technical solutions to audit or compliance problems, at the expense of the more complex process and governance transformation issues that would have driven real change but would have required a longer-term vision and approach.

The technology industry has done little to break those dynamics. In fact, it has been happily riding that wave for a long time, and the trend shows no signs of abating. It also has a long-standing tradition of reinventing itself, and the cybersecurity sector is no exception. Most security vendors are now embracing emerging technologies such as artificial intelligence or machine learning, as well as more established platforms such as big data, and present them as 'innovative' cloud-based delivery models that, in fact, have been in existence – for some of them – for over ten years.

They paint to their clients a situation where threats morph constantly and therefore new tools are constantly required, and it may well be the case to some extent in some industries. But the harsh reality is that many of their clients don't have the basic processes in place that would enable them to take full advantage of such products, and at best, they simply continue to buy those to put ticks in audit or compliance boxes, when it is not merely as a pet project for the CISO.

Many board members have woken up over the past few years to a situation they don't understand, being told all of a sudden that data breaches are simply a matter of time, often by the same people who have been telling them for years that everything was under control.

They need to realise that this is not just an external situation created by the acceleration of threats or some adverse economic or geopolitical outlook. Quite often, it is also the symptom of a serious internal problem rooted in decades of short-termism, adverse prioritisation of security matters, and a complacent 'tick-in-the-box' culture around audit and compliance.

We are coming to a point in many large firms where true 'innovation' in the cybersecurity space does not consist of deploying the latest tools but of going back to the governance drawing board to look at long-term actions and remove the roadblocks that have prevented progress in the past, redesigning fundamental security processes across IT, the business, and other support functions (such as HR) in order to rebuild proper and functional operating models conceived to protect the organisation once and for all.

Cybersecurity in the 'When, not if' Era: No Longer Just as an Equation between Risk Appetite, Compliance Requirements, and Costs

The 'when, not if' paradigm around cyberattacks is changing the deal completely around cybersecurity.

Many large organisations now assume that breaches are simply inevitable, due to the inherent complexity of their business models and the multiplication of attack surfaces and attack vectors that come with it. This realisation fundamentally changes the dynamics around cybersecurity.

Historically, cybersecurity has always been seen as an equation between risk appetite, compliance requirements, and costs. Compliance and costs were always the harder factors. Risk (difficult to measure and quantify) was always some form of adjustment variable.

Risk is about uncertainty. The 'when, not if' paradigm brings certainty where doubt was previously allowed (or used to manipulate outcomes):

- Cyberattacks will happen.
- Sooner or later, regulators will step in.
- They can now impose business-threatening fines around the mishandling of personal data.
- Media interest has never been higher around these matters.
- Business reputation and trust in a brand will be damaged by high-profile incidents.

All the risk-based constructions that have been the foundations of many cybersecurity management practices are weakened as a result.

Compliance requirements remain (if anything, they are getting stronger as privacy regulators flex their muscles in Europe and the United States), and costs cannot be ignored. But 'Are we spending enough?' has become a much more common question across the boardroom table than 'Why do we need to spend so much?'

For CISOs, protecting the firm becomes imperative. This is no longer about doing the minimum required to put the right ticks in compliance boxes, but very often, it is a matter of genuine transformation. It forces them to work across corporate silos, look beyond the mere technology horizon (which is often their comfort zone), and also look beyond tactical firefighting (which often dominates their day-to-day).

Knowing what to do is often the easiest part. After all, good practices in the cybersecurity space have been well known for over a decade, and they still provide adequate protection against many threats – as long as they are properly implemented.

True cyber resilience can only come from real defence-in-depth, acting at preventative, detective, mitigative, and reactive levels – and across the real breadth of the enterprise, functionally and geographically.

The 'when, not if' paradigm will often bring the board's attention and large resources to cybersecurity, but with those will also come scrutiny and expectations. The challenge really becomes an execution and a leadership challenge for the CISO.

In large firms where a major overhaul of security practices is required, establishing a sound governance framework and operating model from the start will always be a key factor of long-term success for the CISO.

Equally important will be the need to put people and process first and to identify the roadblocks that might have prevented progress in the past around cybersecurity matters.

Repeating the mistakes of the past would simply perpetuate the spiral of failure around security, as would an excessive or premature focus on tech solutions. There is no magical technology product that can fix in a few months what is rooted in decades of adverse prioritisation, lip service, and underinvestment. The CISO must appreciate that and place all transformation efforts in the right perspective. Change takes time and relentless drive, and there may not be quick wins.

Managing expectations and staying the course will always be key pillars of any lasting cybersecurity transformation.

Time to Deal with Cybersecurity Strategically and from the Top Down

This is no longer just about tech – if it ever was.

Surveys focused on the concerns and priorities of the CISO community have been quite consistent over the last few years, and collectively, they paint a slightly uncomfortable picture. The picture of CISO roles and security practices still operating bottom-up, disconnected from the dynamics of the business and the broader culture of their organisation.

In spite of the non-stop avalanche of cyberattacks we have seen over the past decade, many CISOs still complain about a lack of board-level engagement and difficulties in getting sufficient budgets.

The overall sentiment is one of frustration, leading to (well-documented) shorter tenures and burnout problems. But another aspect that is often overlooked in the background is the lack of operating structure many cybersecurity practices seem to have.

Instead of being built around some form of operating model that would detail processes, tasks, roles, and responsibilities for all stakeholders, they seem to be driven by projects (in proactive or reactive mode) and operational tasks aggregated over time (exception management for some, privileged access management for others, etc.)

In fact, in the absence of a structured framework to work against, this is often the only way those cybersecurity practices can operate, evolving 'as they go along,' in project mode or in firefighting mode.

Security awareness ends up being a perennial low-hanging fruit and an easy sell for CISOs when they cannot find other levers, but the emphasis on developing a stronger security culture cannot be the only axis of action for the CISO.

But how can you justify budgets and attract or retain talent without a structured referential to work against – and in the absence of a clear governance model, roles, responsibilities, and to a degree (with regard to staff retention), clear career paths?

And again, how can you claim you do not have enough staff in the absence of a target operating model detailing tasks and the resources required to deliver those tasks? It can only be a finger-in-the-air exercise, the very kind any half-decent CFO would smell miles away.

This kind of empirical, bottom-up, and organically developed cybersecurity function does not work. It has failed to protect large organisations over the past two decades and needs to evolve. What is required is structure, business acumen, and top-down engagement.

The culture of frustration many CISOs have developed is probably comfortable for some; there is always someone to blame ('the business') and another juicy job to move into afterwards. But it does not help organisations and society at large. To break this spiral of failure, the profile of the CISO needs to evolve, and the board needs to take ownership.

This is no longer just about tech – if it ever was. This is about protecting the business against cyberattacks that have now become a matter of 'when, not if.' This is no longer something you can push down in the organisation.

If the board does not see the need – or does not feel qualified – to step in, nothing will ever change for good around cybersecurity because it has simply become too complex and too transversal in large organisations. Bottom-up approaches will continue to pour cash down the drain, CISOs will continue to leave every other year out of frustration, and breaches will continue to happen.

If the board wants to set directions, they should drive. They should appoint someone they trust and can talk to (it does not have to be a technologist) and empower that person to build or rebuild cybersecurity practices across the firm, in light of what the board wants and expects.

The COVID crisis has presented most organisations with unprecedented situations, but it has not made cybersecurity less of a priority. On the contrary, cybersecurity – whether it is in support of remote working, e-commerce, or digitalised supply chains – has become a pillar of the 'new normal.'

Now is the time to deal with it strategically, and from the top down.

How Do you Build a Transformational Dynamic?

Security is not about 'enabling' the business but 'protecting' it.

It is true that it is one thing (complex enough) to lead and deliver the cybersecurity transformation of an organisation that has reached the point where it knows it needs to change, but it is another thing (equally complex) to create the condition for such realisation to take place.

Where the business mindset is rooted in short-termism and senior executives are unable to look beyond quick wins and the figures for the next month or the next quarter, how do you get them to the point where they realise that without a greater emphasis on security controls, their business will eventually fall victim to cyber criminals, that cyberattacks are fast becoming a simple matter of when (not if), and that the associated impact (financial and reputational) is increasingly impossible to quantify?

I don't think this is a battle that can be won through a rational engagement. Essentially, it is rooted in breaking down deep cognitive biases, a situation that has been well analysed by Nobel Prize laureate Daniel Kahneman among others.

In a purely bottom-up approach, it is my opinion that many CISOs are simply wasting their time trying to articulate how security could be a 'business enabler,' or trying to calculate some hypothetical 'ROI' on security investments. More often than not, these exercises only add a vernacular of business language over the same old tech storyline, and when it comes to ROI calculations, those are often open to considerable margins of errors or plagued by untested and unverified modelling techniques. It has reached the point where it knows it needs to change, but it is another one – equally complex – to create the condition for such realisation to take place.

This is not the way, in my opinion, you break those cognitive biases, and the problem needs to be approached over time in a completely different manner.

Where security maturity is low but the business is incapable or unwilling to prioritise in favour of much-needed long-term security transformation efforts, the key is for the CISO and the CIO to act at two levels:

First, they must keep their head down and, on a daily basis, continue to deliver on those tactical projects the business wants them to drive. They must be successful at that. They must develop a positive and successful relationship with their business. They must be seen as adding value (whatever value means to the stakeholders).

At the same time, and in parallel to those delivery efforts, they must constantly focus their language towards the business on the reality of the threats it may be facing, not on risks that, ultimately, will always be something that may or may not happen for the business – something you can transfer, mitigate, insure against, not necessarily something you need to do something about.

And they should stay well clear of cliché-esque business jargon ('security as a business enabler!') or business concepts they don't master properly ('ROI of security!').

They should stick to their core competencies (that's where they will be successful) and always bring the discussion back to the field of reality. After all, cyber threats are real, virulent, and targeting almost all business sectors. Cybersecurity doesn't have to excuse itself for existing!

Data breach after data breach, incident after incident, newspaper article after newspaper article, the CISO and the CIO need to push those real life events towards business leaders, picking the right battles and right timing with each executive.

It will require time, political acumen, and a true sense of subtle communication with each business leader, but over time, it will chip away at the defences and create the sense with business leaders that threats are real and internal controls insufficient to ensure adequate protection.

Protecting what you care about is a natural thing for most people, and it should gradually shift priorities towards security matters, to where before they were structurally stacked against those objectives, even in the most complex business situations.

But the CISO and the CIO must also build their own credibility up throughout the exercise, as it is their trustworthiness and ability to deliver the must-needed change that will be tested, and that comes through a demonstrable ability to navigate the political complexity of the firm.

A complex task indeed, in particular in large organisations – not one that needs vague business jargon but strong and determined leadership.

Talent and Governance, not Technology, are Key to Drive Change around Cybersecurity

You are not going to fix your cybersecurity problems simply by buying more tech.

For the last twenty years, large organizations have been spending significant amounts of money on cybersecurity products and solutions, on managed services, or with consultancies large and small.

Yet maturity levels remain elusive: McKinsey surveyed more than 100 firms in 2021 (McKinsey, Organizational cyber maturity: A survey of industries, 2021) and found that 70 percent of their sample 'had yet to fully advance to a mature-based approach'. These results are regularly matched by similar reports and also by the anecdotal evidence we can see in the field every day.

Consensus amongst cybersecurity professionals seems to point towards low maturity levels being a consequence of under-investment in that space.

I have rarely seen that hypothesis thoroughly tested and would argue the problem is broader.

In essence, cybersecurity good practices have been well established for the best part of the last twenty years, and to a large extent, continue to provide in most industries an acceptable level of protection against most threats and an acceptable level of compliance against most regulations.

Over a period of time of such duration, security maturity levels should have developed naturally if they had been carried forward and fostered by genuine business protection values.

Clearly, in many organizations, it has not been the case, or not to a sufficient extent.

In 2019, the Security Transformation Research Foundation conducted a large-scale piece of research analysing the semantic content of 17 Annual Global Security Surveys from EY, looking at the frequency of keywords and the evolution of the language used (STRF, Cyber Security: A Look Across Two Decades, 2019).

The research shows very clearly two decades emerging:

- The first decade of this century, dominated by Risk and Compliance considerations: Security being seen mostly as a balancing act between compliance requirements, risk appetite and costs;
- The second decade of this century, dominated by Threats and Incidents considerations: Security becoming a necessary fire-fighting practice against constant attacks, in a context of massive technological change driven by mobile devices and the Cloud.

None of those are positive drivers: The first one is restrictive, and taken to some extreme, has led to some security practices becoming mere box-checking or window-dressing practices; the second one is short-termist and technology-focused.

More importantly, both isolate cybersecurity from business cycles and business levers.

To me, that's the heart of the matter, and the main reason why maturity levels have remained low in spite of all investments:

Security was always seen as external to the business, locked in a compliance or a technology niche, where it was also alien (compliance and risk people focus on business aspects; technologists have always been incentivized to deliver on features and performance, not on controls).

This is the cultural cycle which has engineered a chronic problem of talent alienation and adverse prioritization, leading to execution failure around security programmes, the historic reluctance of senior executives to commit to large scale investments, and the continuing avalanche of breaches.

Now, things are changing: The 'when, not if' paradigm around cyberattacks has taken root in many boardrooms, and the transformational urgency around cybersecurity practices has been evidenced in many firms by the COVID pandemic and the dependencies it created on digital services.

But it would be a mistake for the board to continue to believe that this is a mere technological problem that is going to be solved just by adding more layers of technology solutions (zero-trust, MFA, AI or whatever it might be).

Key here is to acknowledge the cultural and governance context in which the historic under-achievement of many firms around cybersecurity is rooted.

For genuine and lasting change to take place, cybersecurity now needs to be visibly linked to business values from the board down.

It means cybersecurity ownership being visibly and credibly established at board level, and cybersecurity objectives being visibly and credibly driven from there, injecting raw business talent into the mix by showcasing that success as a cybersecurity transformation agent can be a career accelerator, and that those roles should not be seen as a dead-end or a second best.

For firms genuinely trying to break away from two decades of failure around cybersecurity, talent and governance have to be the real levers, not technology.

The Message That Never Makes It Up to the Board

Cybersecurity was never a purely technical problem; it is now a leadership imperative in many firms.

For the past twenty years, cybersecurity ('information security' in its early days) has been seen primarily as a technical matter, to be solved by technologists using technology means.

In most organisations, it has never been 'owned' as such at board level in spite of the tidal wave of cyberattacks that have rocked most industries across the last decade and the false pretence by many that it's on their agenda.

In reality, it appears periodically at board meetings, sometimes as a matter of good governance pushed by independent directors or auditors and sometimes after an incident or a worrying near-miss.

But generally, it remains an operational matter and somebody else's problem – something the board is concerned about and is supportive of, but something the board is not prepared to consider on its own as board-level material as such.

At best, it has been seen historically as part of the enterprise risk-management practice. Nowadays, with the 'when, not if' paradigm around cyberattacks taking roots, it tends to be seen as part of a broader VUCA agenda, and that is not a bad thing as, indeed, the accumulation of cyberattacks we have been seeing in recent years do form part of those patterns, in particular those that can be related to state-backed actors.

But quite often, there are also concerns about competence around those matters across the boardroom table. Is the board sufficiently digitally savvy to fully appreciate what is at stake and the right actions to take?

These concerns need to be qualified when it comes to cybersecurity. Firstly, because specific competencies can be brought in if required – that's just good governance and something the board can manage. Secondly, because cybersecurity was never a purely technical problem, and that's the message that has failed to make it up to the board over the past decades.

Fundamentally, the time is coming for senior executives to realise that the predominantly technical approach to cybersecurity that has been prevailing over the past two decades – on its own – is failing to protect large organisations from cyberattacks. Not just because cyber threats keep morphing, but because large organisations have become too complex – functionally, geographically, and politically – to effectively deploy protective technical measures across their depth and breadth and across their supply chain, in spite of the billions spent collectively on tech vendors and large consultancies.

Now more than ever, it is dangerous to continue seeing cybersecurity only in its technical dimension. It downgrades the problem and prevents real, long-term solutions from emerging, among other reasons, because it alienates real talent.

Only defence-in-depth can protect large organisations from cyber threats, effectively layering controls at people, process, and technology levels in a structured way, supported by accountabilities and responsibilities spanning the entire enterprise and all its silos (IT, HR, business units, geographies, senior management, etc.).

Putting in place a protective architecture of that type becomes a matter of governance and often requires an amount of culture change around the concepts of control and business protection.

It is not primarily about buying more tech but about the embedding of cybersecurity (i.e., the protection of the business from cyber threats) within a broader controls framework and within the culture of the organisation.

Only top-down dynamics can make this happen, and it is a genuine board-level competency to have the leadership, the gravitas, and the political acumen required to drive it.

Delegating it down to technologists has failed and will continue to fail because most technologists are trained and incentivised to deliver on functionality and efficiency, not on culture change or control mindset.

The board has no reason to feel embarrassed in taking ownership of what has become, fundamentally, a leadership matter in most firms – in particular where cyber maturity is low and urgent transformation is required. It is the only way to make it happen.

Turning the Tables on Cybersecurity Budgets

Time to move away from bottom-up dynamics: The board should decide on priorities and drive the discussion.

As we hit budget time again in many large organisations, it is still amazing to see the amount of content online dedicated to justifying cybersecurity investments or convincing the board.

This is difficult to match with field experience. As we have been saying repeatedly since 2019, the penny has dropped or is dropping in many boardrooms, in the face of the non-stop epidemic of cyberattacks we have seen over the past decade, which was even aggravated by the COVID crisis.

Cyberattacks are now seen as a matter of when, not if. This is no longer, strictly speaking, a matter of risk (something that may or may not happen and has a probability of occurrence) but a matter of certainty, and as a result, the attitude of senior executives has shifted with regard to cybersecurity.

Today questions around 'Are we spending enough on cyber?' are more common across the boardroom than 'Why do we need to spend so much?'

In many large organisations, the board no longer needs convincing that cybersecurity investments are required. The board needs to be given assurances that delivery and execution will follow, and in that respect, quite a lot of the arguments developed online around the topic seem to be going back several decades.

Board members and senior executives 'have been there before' with cyber investment plans. Many large organisations would have spent millions or tens of millions with tech vendors and large consultancies over the past two decades, just to see a fresh-faced CISO (often the last one in a long line) coming back and asking for more money to buy more tech, arguing that threats keep morphing and that the world is about to end unless they buy more tech – all that backed by endless reports from tech vendors and their pet consultants.

CISOs – in particular, incoming CISOs – have to change their narrative to avoid unnecessary discussions. This is no longer about risk reduction or ROI with the board. In real terms, those ships have sailed long ago ... and CISOs facing those types of questions must ask themselves the hard questions and face why.

The focus since the start of the COVID crisis has been on tactical and technical initiatives around cybersecurity, but those are rarely truly transformative, and many would just have added various layers of tech legacy on top of already-crowded security estates.

CISOs must start focusing on softer matters and showcase their ability to execute, because the priorities have to be on protecting the business now and in the longer term from real and imminent threats.

It has to start by demonstrating a sense of context, both in terms of business cycles and security investment cycles. Very few organisations are pure green fields in terms of cybersecurity, and almost always, there will be a legacy of cybersecurity investments and practices to deal with. What happened to the last investments? Were they rightly targeted? What did they achieve (or failed to achieve)? What has prevented sufficient progress?

Showing an understanding of where roadblocks have been in the past, looking over the right time frames, and focusing on transformative initiatives that can actually be delivered in real life, given the business context and the available skills and resources, should be key to convince the board that new forces are at play and that a transformative dynamic is being established to avoid repeating the mistakes of the past.

This is likely to take the CISO into the fields of governance and culture, not technology (both within IT and the business), and those themes should resonate with the board and give them something they can relate to and address. Because fundamentally, this is what matters most.

The board needs to take ownership of the real cybersecurity agenda and start driving it from the top down, at their level, in terms they can understand and manage, removing roadblocks and looking beyond tech and pure tech matters driven bottom-up.

From that point, it should no longer be a matter of convincing the board of anything around cyber but of delivering on what they expect.

The Four Pillars of a Lasting Cybersecurity Transformation

Simply throwing money at the problem is rarely the answer.

Many CIOs and CISOs would have come across this situation after an incident, a serious near-miss, or a bad audit report. Suddenly, money and resources – which were previously scarce – appear out of nowhere, priorities shift, and senior executives demand urgent action around cybersecurity.

It is probably the dream of many CISOs to inherit one day such a transformational challenge where money is, apparently, no object. In practice, however, it can also be a curse if you fail to deliver.

What are the key factors in driving successful transformation around cybersecurity?

1. Setting the Right Time Frames

First, the CISO must assess without complacency the true nature of the transformation required, the depth of commitment of senior management, and the time frames that would be required to deliver real and lasting change – independent of stakeholders' expectations.

This is the first area where the CISO will need to manage expectations with senior executives. Change takes 'the time it takes,' in particular where culture and behaviours are involved, and some aspects associated with cybersecurity transformation could be complex, disturb existing business practices, and lead to substantial projects (e.g., around identity and access management or data leak prevention).

In our experience, the complete top-down reengineering of an entire security practice can take up to three to five years in any large organisation. Nobody can be expected to achieve anything significant in six months to a year if initial maturity levels are very low; two years may not be enough either.

The first management challenge of the CISO is to get senior stakeholders to understand that fact. This is about a real commitment to change at least as much as it is about resources and the ability to think strategically over the medium to long term. Not all senior executives or board members are capable of doing that. The CISO will have to find the right allies and use their influence to get the message across.

Merely 'fixing' illusory quick wins never amounts to lasting transformation.

The realisation of the time frames involved will be rooted in the appreciation by senior management of the tasks involved, and such appreciation needs to be backed against a sound and meaningful assessment of the starting point.

From there, a transformative vision and road map can be drawn by looking towards the right horizon.

2. Focusing on Clear Transformative Themes and Explicit Goals

In situations where the organisation needs to face fundamental change around cybersecurity, it will be essential to set clear and simple objectives for all parties.

Trying to fix everything at the same time, irrespective of interdependencies, the inherent complexity of some issues, and possibly over unrealistic time frames will simply lead to confusion and failure.

Instead, the CISO should start by assessing dependencies between the various parts of the transformative road map and group action around broad themes, which in turn, will focus on priorities and investments.

Those themes should be clear, simple to articulate, and structured around explicit goals and milestones.

3. Delivering through an Empowered Senior Team

Although there will be projects involved in delivering the transformative road map, the ultimate objective is to create a sustainable and self-standing transformed security practice. To this end, the reengineering of their team needs to be the first task for the CISO so that transformation can be delivered through the reshaped team and not only through contingent project resources and consultants.

Defining the right team structure and operating and governance model should be a top priority for the CISO, involving all relevant stakeholders across IT, business, and support functions and also involving all relevant geographies and third parties.

Staffing the new team should follow and start top-down so that the CISO can delegate the transformative burden to empowered senior direct reports. This layer of management, once established, will take on the duties to staff the rest of their teams and deliver explicit parts of the transformative road map. Finding those people – internally or externally – in the current recruitment market could be tough and take time, so starting as early as possible in this phase should be key for the CISO.

From there, the delivery of the transformative road map can start, but it will be equally crucial for the CISO to ensure that all key personnel are incentivised to stay the course as there may be rough waters ahead.

4. Sticking to the Plan

Establishing realistic time frames, setting clear goals, and finding the right people to drive the transformative efforts through a structured team are key. In parallel, the CISO should continue to get all parties on board behind the right transformative road map. This phase could easily take up to six months, but it is essential to long-term success.

There may be quick wins, or there may not be. The CISO must resist inventing some where there are none and must also avoid knee-jerk reactions that may only damage the long-term case.

One thing this is not about is implementing more tech – at least not upfront.

There is no magical technology platform or service provider that can be, on its own, the answer to a fundamental transformative challenge around cybersecurity.

Technology will, of course, have a role to play in the transformative effort in most organisations, but the CISO and their team must come to that in due course and, in the right context, set up the right transformative vision, road map, and operating model. Jumping at tech solutions and tech vendors upfront cannot be the first thing to do.

The overarching challenge for the CISO behind all this lies in getting senior management to see that a long-term change is rooted in a long-term vision and long-term planning that takes time to establish.

It may be a hard sell in the absence of tactical quick wins, and a lot will rest on the trust between the CISO and their boss, as well as the personal profile, managerial experience, and political acumen of the CISO.

Given the complexities involved, which are not just technical but also often rooted in culture and governance, delivering lasting change will always require a structured approach and a relentless drive to succeed.

Simply throwing money at the problem in the hope of making it disappear, without proper consideration of those matters, simply leads to failure and can only aggravate the perception of the senior stakeholders that security is just a cost and a burden.

In Defence of Maturity-Based Approaches for Cybersecurity

It Doesn't Make Sense to Oppose Maturity- and Risk-Based Approaches to Cybersecurity

The assumption that risk-based approaches are somehow more advanced than maturity-based ones and represent an 'evolution' of cybersecurity practices is highly disputable, and the quantification put forward by McKinsey in 2019 of maturity-based approaches as leading to overengineering and overspending by a factor three compared to risk-based approaches is simply misleading (a footnote in their article actually refers to the costs mentioned as 'illustrative and extrapolated from real-world examples and estimates') (McKinsey, 2019).

As a matter of fact, those two approaches are just different ways of managing, driving, and measuring action around cybersecurity in different situations and different firms. One does not have to be superior to the other.

The keys are elsewhere: The approach one firm decides to follow has to be right in relation to the firm's management and governance culture and its objectives around cybersecurity. Those will vary naturally from one organization to another, and from one management team to the next.

One trend we are observing more and more is actually the weakening of traditional risk and compliance drivers around cybersecurity with senior executives. The 'when, not if' paradigm around cyberattacks is strongly taking root in many boardrooms, and many firms are committing very large amounts to large-scale transformative security programmes. But in return, the board expects execution and protection, and they are holding CIOs and CISOs accountable for both.

In those situations, risk often goes to the background, delivery takes centre stage, and maturity-based approaches generally work well – as long as they revolve around a clear set of capabilities to be developed through the delivery of clear, tangible actions to achieve a clear target maturity level.

This is not an approach that will work well only in situations where initial maturity levels are low. It can continue to work throughout the maturity spectrum up to advanced levels. As long as the capabilities and actions required to develop them are backed against the firm's objective around cybersecurity and the real threats it is facing, there is no reason to assume that it would lead to a greater degree of overengineering – and overspending – compared to other approaches.

As a matter of fact, whether a firm takes a maturity-driven route or a risk-driven one to ensure it is well protected from cyber threats, none of that changes the nature, reality, and virulence of those threats and, as a result, the nature of the measures the firm needs to have in place to be well protected. Those necessary protective measures may end up ordered or prioritised differently, in order to improve maturity or reduce risk, but barring political manipulation by stakeholders, they will be the same and will cost the same.

The chosen approach simply needs to be right to give the executives in charge the levers they need to understand and manage the firm's cybersecurity posture.

It is our experience that simplicity, clarity, and consistency are often the real factors behind successful approaches, and at that game, maturity-based models often win because they can be action-driven from the start, faster to put in place, and less vulnerable to window-dressing by stakeholders.

The Way Forward with Cybersecurity Target Operating Models

Many large organisations across all industries face the same challenges around cybersecurity and privacy:

- Growing regulatory demands compounded by escalating cyber threats and skills shortages and;

- A business landscape dominated by the COVID pandemic and its economic and geopolitical aftermath.

Very often, their cybersecurity operating model has simply grown organically over the years and needs reengineering or restructuring to bring it in line with evolving regulatory frameworks, align it with the industry's best practices in terms of three lines of defence and risk management, and fundamentally give senior executives assurance that their business remains adequately protected from cyber threats across people, process, and technology levels.

So what are the best ways to move forward with a cybersecurity operating model reengineering programme?

First of all, it is key to accept that the main challenges in delivering a new operating model will be leadership challenges. Creating an effective cybersecurity practice often stems from driving cultural and governance changes across an organisation. It requires a coherent leadership vision, long-term action, and a relentless drive to succeed.

That's why the approach to building the new operating model must be as interactive and iterative as possible. Engaging with all stakeholders and getting them on board from the start is key as, going forward, they will have to live the values of the TOM and make it happen in real life.

Also another key is understanding that a radical shake-up of approaches around cybersecurity (if that's what's required) cannot be driven simply bottom-up, or horizontally, across the business. It needs a top-down element to succeed. In that respect, a clear endorsement from senior stakeholders is also essential before the new operating model is taken to its actors for validation and implementation. Quite often, the involvement of HR will also be required if organisational arrangements or job descriptions have to change. (In some geographies or industries, employee representatives, trade unions, or workers' councils may also have to be informed or consulted.)

Finally, all too often, we see those projects failing on excessive complexity and internal politics. Simplicity, clarity, and transparency of objectives are always the best success factors in any new operating model implementation.

A cybersecurity TOM has to be seen as a high-level description of the operational processes that need to be in place across the cybersecurity team, the business, and the support functions to ensure adequate and regulatory-compliant protection of the organisation from cyber threats. The TOM is implemented through an organisational model, which documents specific roles (through role descriptions), accountabilities, and responsibilities (through an overall RACI mapping) for all the people involved in the delivery of the TOM.

Going forward, it is the new leadership structure defined as part of the new organisational model that needs to take ownership in building up action plans to deliver on the actual alignment of their respective practices with the process content of the TOM (each depending on the specific level of maturity of their area). It is in that context that they should drive the selection of the relevant technology products and service providers to help them with that.

There is no need for specific technical requirements to be an integral part of the TOM itself, which should remain a governance framework.

Regulatory frameworks (such as NIS, PCI DSS, GDPR, etc.) must inform the TOM, which in turn must contain the right process components to ensure that the relevant technical aspects coming from those regulations are embedded in technical policies, procedures, and standards and are properly implemented within critical systems.

A review of the content of technical policies, procedures, and standards may be required as part of the implementation of the new TOM to ensure all regulatory requirements are captured, and the TOM should also ensure that a process is in place to periodically review the technical compliance of critical systems against all the regulatory frameworks and internal policies they need to comply with.

'Process and people first, then technology' will always be at the heart of the winning formula here – technology to support a structured set of processes that enable people to protect the business from cyber threats.

The 'Three Lines of Defence' Model
Only Works on Trust

It is no big secret that the 'three lines of defence' model underpinning many GRC practices in large firms is poorly understood and poorly applied at grassroots levels.

Anecdotal evidence we observe in the field every day suggests that many organisations operate it in a variety of hybrid fashions, knowingly or unknowingly, and they experience a range of dysfunctions that seriously limit the value the model is designed to bring.

These dysfunctions all revolve around the same problem in our experience: a form of defiance between the parties that builds up over time and is rooted in inconsistencies, lack of clarity around reporting models, language issues, and a lack of overarching investment coherence at board level.

For example, it is not uncommon to find situations where first-line controls are fundamentally weak or missing in some areas. This is something the second line must identify and report on, but at the same time, the second line cannot become prescriptive with regard to the implementation of the relevant first-line controls (even if the actual nature of the second-line controls themselves may always influence the determination of the first-line controls to be put in place). It is unavoidable, in those situations, that first-line stakeholders may feel singled out and exposed, particularly in the following instances:

- Those deficiencies are going to be reported in the simplistic format of a RAG report to a body of management where they are not represented.

- The topic at hand is genuinely complex, multidimensional, and rooted in decades of adverse legacy (and may be impossible to explain in simple terms to senior executives coming from a totally different background).

- The same issues were not identified in an earlier targeted audit performed by the third line.

Their management is clearly pushing them towards other priorities, sometimes coupled with aggressive cost reductions.

It is easy to look at this list and think that most of it revolves around ordinary, day-to-day political dysfunctions that are common to many large firms and impossible to avoid to a large extent. After all, the 'three lines of defence' model is not designed to avoid those issues but to highlight them so that they can be treated (maybe).

But it remains unavoidable that, over time, these dynamics create the conditions for distrust to build up at the interface between the lines of defence, in particular if personalities don't match or where differences in personal backgrounds create language issues or other barriers.

Distrust breeds window dressing, and in the long run, it could bring data quality or relevance issues that may seriously skew risk reporting and mislead investors or shareholders.

These situations are generally hard to unlock, with second- and third-line functions often entrenched in dogmatic separation-of-duties considerations.

There are two lines of action to treat the problem:

- Heads of risk, compliance, or internal audit should ensure that counterparts across the lines come from a similar background and professional culture. For example, the second- or third-line staff should have faced the same day-to-day challenges as their first-line counterparts at some point in their career and should, therefore, relate to those more naturally and more practically. Using only lifelong auditors or lifelong consultants to staff those layers often creates the conditions highlighted above.

- Where first-line maturity is really low towards controls and first-line stakeholders are genuinely struggling with the concepts involved, heads of risk, compliance, or internal audit should sponsor the setup of a separate 'controls architecture' function (independent from their respective teams) that would assist stakeholders in that respect.

Separation of duties is important, and it is often looked at dogmatically by regulators. But an overarching principle of efficiency has to prevail, in particular where senior management is genuinely driving a culture of change around controls. In an earlier post, we have highlighted how this principle of efficiency could be applied (e.g., where the InfoSec function is structured within the portfolio of the CIO).

Hybrid models can work and bring value around GRC – more than watertight and dogmatic separated models – but as long as the dynamics of trust and efficiency are preserved.

The CISO Must Be – First and Foremost – a Leader

The key challenges of the transformational CISO are not technological but managerial.

There is still a vast amount of debate across the cybersecurity industry about the role of the CISO, their reporting line, their tenure, the levels of stress they're under, and the burnout epidemy they're suffering.

But looking into the actual profile of real people in those jobs, talking to them and listening to their problems, you'd quickly realise that there is a fair amount of creative writing involved in a lot that's being posted.

It is easy to write about 'the CISO,' thinking this is a fully established C-level role and one of the pillars of corporate governance. In practice, this is far from being the case, and the harsh reality is that the role itself is far from mature – in spite of having been in existence, in some shape or another, for about two decades.

The job title – to start with – is far from universal (and has never been). A large number of variants are in use, and behind those are different role descriptions reflecting the perceptions and priorities of each organisation, which in turn find themselves reflected in the reporting line of the function.

Compounded by the natural differences between industry sectors and the security maturity levels of each company, it creates a myriad of roles – which, in the end, can have very little in common.

The reality of the role of a 'CISO' reporting to a board member in a mining firm will have very little to do with the role of a 'CISO' reporting two levels below the CIO in a retail organisation. Even if good practices are the same – and have been for a long time, and they still protect – putting them in place in each of those situations will have very different meanings.

So talking about 'the CISO' is often a dangerous shortcut when trying to address the functional or operational aspects of the role.

The commonalities are to be found around the softer aspects of the role.

First of all, if an organisation is large enough to frame the role in CISO terms, it is likely the CISO will have a team below them. This is where many articles on the theme often go wrong. They talk about 'the CISO' as if he or she was a one-man (one-woman) band, directly involved in the delivery of all aspects of their cybersecurity practice. That's rarely the case. In most organisations, the CISO is effectively a leader – structuring, organising, delegating, and orchestrating work across their team, the firm, and the multiple third parties involved in delivering or supporting the business.

The CISO should also be expected to be able to listen to business leaders across corporate silos, understand their priorities, and adjust security practices to their demands and expectations.

It is simply absurd to pretend that the CISO should have those managerial skills and at the same time expect them to constantly put out burning fires and be credible all the time – all the way across all technical stacks and across all silos of a large corporate. These unicorn profiles simply don't exist.

What is not absurd is to expect the CISO to structure and lead a team that can be credible on all those fronts, firefight, and bring along long-term change. That's the only way it can work in large firms.

Senior executives also need to understand the complexities involved in leading true security transformation across large corporates and accept the gaps that may exist at times between knowing what needs to be done to protect the business, saying it should be done, and making sure it gets done for good and across the real breadth and depth of the enterprise.

In bridging those gaps lie the real challenges of the role of the transformational CISO. Those are not technological challenges but managerial, political, and governance challenges.

To be successful, the transformational CISO needs to be – first and foremost – a leader with a good business brain, not just a firefighting technologist.

Getting Things Done: The Secret Sauce for the CISO

Looking beyond its reasons, the short tenure of the CISO raises another question:

What do you actually achieve in two or three years in a complex and transversal field such as cybersecurity and, in particular, in large firms?

One of my readers pointed out that some CISOs work precisely on those patterns because they are hired to put specific compliance-alignment programmes in place, and they leave when the job is done, which typically involves those two- to three-year time frames.

But what happens next? What guarantees can the business have that the next CISO will follow in the footsteps of the previous one? There are many ways to interpret and execute compliance requirements, and no doubt every cybersecurity professional has specific areas of expertise and particular pet subjects. It is not easy to step in and execute a programme of work designed by someone else. Because in my view, the key around cybersecurity remains execution, execution, and execution.

Knowing what to do is reasonably well established, and good cybersecurity practice at large still protects from most threats and still ensures a degree of compliance with most regulations. Putting it in place in real life, across the depth and breadth of the modern enterprise, is exactly where large firms have failed over the past twenty years in spite of the colossal investments in that space with tech vendors and large consultancies.

Large organisations morph constantly, either through mergers, organic expansion, or their digital transformation (not mentioning major disruptive global events such as the 2008–2009 financial crisis or the COVID pandemic). Business priorities and perceptions of risk shift accordingly, and they mechanically follow business cycles (long or short) and the visibility those cycles can afford business leaders at any given time. Those dynamics are unavoidable.

But cybersecurity works on different patterns – in particular where maturity is low and real change is required to face escalating threats.

Very often, past execution failure in that space has left scars on senior executives. Some would have seen several generations of CISOs coming in with a grandiose transformative plan asking for millions, before disappearing after a few years having achieved very little in practice in terms of real change.

The secret sauce for new CISOs will be in demonstrating that they can get things done over the right time frames by manoeuvring around the political maze of large organisations and understanding how they really operate.

This is rarely about buying more tech but more about understanding where the roadblocks are that have prevented progress in the past (and how they link with the business culture of the firm) and working out ways to remove or circumnavigate them.

It requires real life managerial experience, personal gravitas, and political acumen – more than raw technical skills – because the CISO will not deliver change on their own and cannot be expected to.

They will do it by leading a team of experts, influencing change, and driving the execution of protective measures across the organisation and its supply chain.

More than ever, the key issue for the transformational CISO is time. It takes 'the time it takes' to build the right team and drive the long-term dynamics of change around cybersecurity practices, across a more and more complex business environment also changing all the time, possibly on different cycles.

As well as business cycles, CISOs must be realistic around the perspective they give themselves to achieve change in order to place their role on the right trajectory over the medium to long term; they must also be allowed and incentivised by their business to do so.

This is much harder than it might have been ten or fifteen years ago, when the enterprise was more self-contained. To keep a bond of trust with senior stakeholders, they must focus all the time on getting things done, not just over the short term, as inevitably, tactical initiatives and firefighting requirements will emerge, but also strategically over the medium to long term as part of a structured and coherent vision for business protection endorsed by all from the board down.

Leading by Listening: The Other Secret Sauce for the CISO

In the face of non-stop cyberattacks, and the urgency of change around cybersecurity practices in large firms, the role of the CISO can no longer be limited to its technical content.

Cybersecurity has a technical dimension, of course, and a fundamental one; but it was never just about tech.

Delivering real and lasting change around cybersecurity across the complexity of large organisations has to involve all corporate silos: business units, geographies and support functions, as well as IT and suppliers. Bringing them all on board with a common and coherent cybersecurity agenda cannot be something arbitrary or predetermined.

It can only be built on the basis of the situation and priorities of all stakeholders. They will buy into it if there is something in it for them; they will resent it and drag their feet if it comes across as something arbitrary imposed by the head office.

So understanding the firm's governance dynamics – and frankly, the internal politics – will be key for the CISO in large organisations to calibrate the change agenda to a level the fabric of the business can tolerate. That has to start by listening to key stakeholders, understanding their challenges and priorities around cybersecurity, as well as the general situation of the business.

The times have gone when the CISO had to explain what cybersecurity was about and the value it brought. All business leaders would have been exposed to the concept of cyber threats and cyberattacks given the level of media coverage over the last decade. Many would have faced their impact in other roles. They will have a view on the matter and, quite often, a balanced business view of what to do – or not to do – about it.

Too many CISOs jump straight at technical recipes or try to apply ready-made solutions they have used or seen elsewhere.

'What can I do to help you?' should be the opening question for the CISO in their exchanges with stakeholders.

Listening to the answers, accepting them for what they are (irrespective of the CISO's personal inclinations), structuring them into a strategic change agenda, and most importantly, delivering on the expectations created are the pillars on which a successful CISO should build their practice (in particular the incoming CISO).

At this point, we start to see emerging a profile of a certain type for the CISO that will be key for the role to be successful. The profile of an individual who has sufficient management experience and political acumen to navigate the complex governance waters of large firms, the ability to listen without jumping to a predetermined agenda, and the ability to deliver on expectations in a complex and transversal field.

Where maturity is low and aggressive change is required around cybersecurity practices, those attributes are more important, in my view, than the native ability to understand the technology context in which cybersecurity is rooted.

Of course, these are attributes that some technologists can develop naturally over the course of a career in tech (in particular in senior roles). But fundamentally, they are leadership attributes that come with time and experience.

The key for me is the quality of listening and building some realistic and achievable consensus around the expectations collected from stakeholders, without always dropping to the lowest common denominator (generally, that's awareness development in the cybersecurity space – whatever that means in practice).

It's a difficult task, but it is the essence of true leadership. Going back to the basic meaning of the word, a leader is someone who is followed, and people generally follow when they have the sense that they will get something in return.

These are the simple dynamics successful CISOs have to build around cybersecurity.

The Momentum Behind the Role of the Chief Security Officer

In many large organizations, defining and structuring a Chief Security Officer role (CSO) is starting to make more and more sense.

The concept is not new and has generally been used to encompass all security aspects a firm may be faced with – physical and digital.

It is time to look at it under a broader angle in many large companies.

Broadly speaking, the role of the CISO (Chief Information Security Officer) has failed to drive change and build sufficient momentum around cybersecurity issues over the last two decades.

This is mostly driven by an excessive technological focus, that has imprisoned the CISOs in technical firefighting and prevented them from adequately reaching across the business and developing sufficient management and political acumen.

Today, as the penny is dropping across boardrooms, and the 'when, not if' paradigm dominates around cyberattacks, they are trapped in an impossible role where it is expected of them to be audible and credible across the depth and breadth of the enterprise, from boards and regulators, to pen testers and developers.

No profile can reach effectively across a spectrum of skills that wide, and it starts to make sense to evolve the role by separating the components it has been accumulating over the years.

This is made all the more important by the increasing regulatory and reporting pressure, which has been mounting steadily for all businesses over the past decade across all industry sectors: It started around data privacy with the GDPR in Europe and many equivalent state regulations in the U.S. Reporting demands are now developing at federal level, and governance aspects are also coming under increased scrutiny.

This regulatory intervention is simply the result of devastating cyberattacks, that have threatened or impacted key infrastructure components, and brought under broad daylight the extent of the disruption those types of events can cause.

As a result, senior executives have started to look beyond traditional business continuity approaches, to pay more and more attention to resilience concepts.

All those aspects (cybersecurity, regulatory compliance, resilience) have one major component in common: They are cross-functional and require a reach across corporate silos to be effective and efficient.

I would add that on those three fronts, the risk dimension is increasingly becoming obsolete in my opinion: This is no longer about events that may or may not happen, but simply a business reality that has to be factored in the way the firm operates.

Those are the factors combining to build momentum behind a redefined role for the CSO, encompassing oversight of physical and cybersecurity, but also data privacy, operational resilience and their associated compliance and regulatory reporting obligations.

A role of that magnitude in most firms can only make sense and function from the top of the firm, as part of the most senior business leadership team.

It has to be seen as a senior management role, focused on building the necessary cross-functional channels, ensuring they remain active, and bridging across business and political issues by bringing sufficient gravitas and credibility around the matters involved.

It is – of course – a role for a seasoned executive, motivated overall by the protection of the business from active threats, able to take an elevated long-term view where required, over and above the short-term fluctuations of any business.

We are miles away from the current role of most CISOs (our starting point), but it does not make their job any less relevant.

To the contrary, it offers an opportunity to refocus the role of the CISO on its native technical content and give it a renewed currency by stripping off the corporate layers added over the years, for which its holders – most of them technologists by trade or background – were poorly prepared.

A dual reporting line to both the CSO and the CIO would then make sense for the CISO and ensure a degree of independent oversight in industries where those aspects around separation of duties are scrutinised.

This type of model is essential in my view to drive large-scale programmes, where cybersecurity maturity is low and urgent transformation is required across the cybersecurity practices of an organisation.

The combination of the top-down and cross-functional influence of the CSO with the technical reach of the CISO should be key to create and maintain the momentum required to deliver change, and break business resistance where it happens.

Going the Right Way about Cybersecurity Transformation

This interesting piece in the Harvard Business Review should be a must-read for all transformational CISOs (HBR, The Most Successful Approaches to Leading Organizational Change, 2023)

Its focus on the true dynamics of change, and the fact that change leaders focus too much on the 'what' of change and not the 'how', bring out obvious parallels with situations we are seeing all too often in the field around cybersecurity transformation.

Irrespective of their original level of cyber maturity, most organisations have the tendency to treat cybersecurity transformation as a controllable, straightforward type of change, warranting directive approaches.

In keeping with the purely technical and operational focus that has been plaguing cybersecurity approaches for decades, transformation is often architected around projects and the deployment of tools. Stakeholders are broadly told what to do and are expected to follow rules; if and when they don't, this is pinned down to lack of 'training' or 'awareness'; two other projects and low hanging fruits many CISOs are keen to regard as the alpha and omega of cybersecurity.

This culture of 'blaming the user' is regressive, and in the end, all this is rarely transformative in itself: Projects are vulnerable to adverse prioritisation and are often reshaped as business priorities evolve. More often than not, they do not deliver on their primary objectives in a way that would match initial expectations.

Engineering true dynamics of change around cybersecurity has to start with two essential steps:

First of all, the proper examination of past failed approaches or initiatives in that space.

Although cybersecurity has been making significant gains in visibility at top level over the past few years, it did not appear on the board's agenda out of thin air and has been evolving for over two decades. Examining without complacency what might have gone wrong in the past and confronting the true roadblocks that would have prevented change to stick, is a fundamental prerequisite.

This is likely to lead cybersecurity transformation leaders towards cultural and governance issues, as well as possible under investments.

Often, the latter (under investments) is simply a symptom of the former (cultural and governance issues) and is easily illustrated by situations where money – which was previously denied – appears out of nowhere at the first sight of an incident, a near-miss, a regulatory visit or simply a bad audit report.

Confronting those types of cognitive biases – or at least acknowledging them – is essential in understanding the dynamics of change around cybersecurity.

This is where many training and awareness programs go wrong: They frame the argument as a rational argument – something that has to be explained or taught – instead of focusing on the deeper cultural issues at the heart of the matter.

This is taking us to our second essential step: The need to acknowledge cybersecurity as a cross-functional discipline and to build trust with all stakeholders.

Nothing lasting can happen in that space without listening first to all the parties that have a role to play in protecting the business from cyber threats, understanding their constraints, their fears, their priorities, and where they might see conflicts around the objectives of the cybersecurity transformation programme.

There cannot be any more fundamental aspect in engineering true dynamics of change around cybersecurity.

Imposing new measures or practices onto stakeholders without prior engagement and a true exchange of views simply creates friction, and over time, rejection or cynicism in the face of endless rules. Overall, it breeds frustration and incomprehension around what cybersecurity is about.

Going back to the language of the authors in our starting article, the combination of 'emergent' and 'masterful' change driven top-down by senior executives is likely to be the best blend for cybersecurity transformation ('creating the conditions for change' and 'trusting people to deliver'), as is often the case for any type of complex change.

That's the main point: Cybersecurity transformation cannot be seen as a straightforward change; cybersecurity transformation is complex and transversal and needs to be treated as such in all its dimensions.

Conclusion

. . . .

Why Cybersecurity is Now a Board-Level Leadership Imperative

Supporting cybersecurity and promoting it has now become a plain matter of good leadership.

We are not hearing enough about the short tenure of the CISO.

Regular studies place it in the region of two years, and anecdotal evidence from my own network, based on the analysis of the profile of 15 current CISOs, points towards 30 months.

In my opinion, it is often the symptom of serious underlying issues and the cornerstone of long-term stagnation for many cybersecurity practices in large firms.

We have to look beyond the most commonly invoked reasons: Lack of resources, disconnect with management, and constant firefighting leading to mental health issues and burnout.

All three aspects, in my opinion, point towards the profile of the CISOs themselves.

Not all organisations are doing well and not all organisations are well managed, but it is hard to imagine one where senior executives and board members would be insensitive to cybersecurity issues, given the level of media coverage of the past decade and the non-stop occurrence of cyberattacks.

Actually, 'are we spending enough on cyber?' has become a far more common question at these levels over recent years, than 'why do we need to spend so much?'

In such context, CISOs failing to obtain the resources they deem necessary to do their job, should ask themselves where this is going wrong.

More often than not, the problem is rooted, not so much in the amounts involved or the storytelling by the CISOs, but in the excessively technical focus of the demands, and the trust deposited by senior executives in the CISOs themselves with regards to their ability to execute on what they are asking.

Let's not forget that the role of the CISO is rarely a board-level construction engineered top-down; at best, it has evolved bottom-up out of a technical context; in most cases, it is still a technical construction rooted in IT matters.

Over the past decade, many senior executives and board members in large firms would have seen several generations of CISOs coming up with grandiose plans asking for millions to spend on tech firms and tech products, before disappearing after a few years having achieved very little in practice.

It is hard to get things done in real terms in large firms on a complex topic such as cybersecurity, which cuts across all corporate silos, in particular where maturity levels are low and radical change is required. It requires time, persistence, and relentless drive.

On cybersecurity matters, the penny has dropped years ago in the boardroom around the 'when, not if' paradigm, but CISOs need to understand how much this is changing the nature of the agenda for senior executives.

All of sudden, this is no longer just about risk – something which may or may not happen – or putting ticks in compliance boxes at minimal cost; it becomes a plain matter of business protection and as a result, the actual execution of protective measures becomes paramount.

But CISOs have been poorly prepared by the last decade for the type of management challenges involved in this shift.

They continue to understand 'when, not if' as meaning 'whatever-we-do-we-will-be-breached' and to see the value they bring as being rooted simply in the short-term tactical and technical firefighting of cyberattacks, and not so much in the actual implementation of good practices with the view of delivering a degree of long-term and lasting protection across the firm.

That's the root of the disconnect between CISOs and many senior executives: They are often prepared to consider large investments around cybersecurity, but they expect to be given a sense of perspective, credible execution to follow, and some degree of protection to result from it; not just constant demands to buy more tech, covered in technical jargon, every time something happens …

All this breeds frustration; frustration breeds mutual distrust; distrust breeds unwillingness to commit resources; this is the vicious circle which feeds short tenures.

In practice, short tenures breed long-term stagnation: You don't achieve a lot in large firms in two to three years; quite often, very little gets done beyond tactical measures and alleged technical low-hanging fruits; almost always, projects which have started are aborted or left unfinished, as the next CISO has other views, or business priorities have changed.

To break this spiral of failure, in particular where maturity is low and things need to change, the board needs to take ownership, assign clear responsibility for cybersecurity to a senior executive they trust at their level, and start driving the topic top-down with a sense of long-term perspective, looking beyond the day-to-day of the business.

Board members often object that they simply don't have the skills to do that, but in my opinion, it is a misconception, and they must not stop at that hurdle: Cybersecurity is not just a technology problem; it never was.

It is a problem rooted in culture and governance, which happens to have a technology dimension like almost everything large enterprises do.

Getting the governance right from the top down around cybersecurity is a plain leadership matter which fits perfectly in a board agenda, and the necessary start to embed the right business protection culture in each and every corporate silo.

Middle management needs to see the right attitude, the right example and the right message coming consistently from the top around cybersecurity, and in most cases, given the right support, they will follow.

Good cybersecurity is quite simply good business; it protects the firm and its customers and builds resilience; supporting it and promoting it has now become a plain matter of good leadership.

About the Author

· ·

Jean-Christophe Gaillard

JC Gaillard is the Founder and CEO of Corix Partners, a London-based Boutique Management Consultancy Firm and Thought-Leadership Platform, focused on assisting CIOs and other C-level executives in resolving Cybersecurity Strategy, Organisation and Governance challenges.

He is a leading strategic advisor and a globally-recognised cybersecurity thought-leader with over twenty-five years of experience developed in several financial institutions in the UK and continental Europe, and a track-record at driving fundamental change in the Security field across global organisations, looking beyond the technical horizon into strategy, governance, culture, and the real dynamics of transformation.

French and British national permanently established in the UK since 1993, he holds an Engineering Degree from Telecom Paris and has been co-president of the Cybersecurity group of the Telecom Paris alumni association since May 2016.

He runs the Corix Partners blog and the 'Security Transformation Leadership' publication on Medium.

He is a Fellow of the Chartered Institute of Information Security (FCIIS), a member of the Forbes Business Council and contributes regularly to the London Tech Leaders and TechNative websites; he has also posted regularly in the past on the Business Transformation Network, The Digital Transformation People, IoTforAll, Business 2 Community and Experfy platforms.

He is an expert contributor on the CIO Water Cooler, and has previously published articles on InfoSecurity Magazine, Computing, the C-Suite.co.uk, Info Sec Buzz, Disruption Hub, and the IoD Director websites.

He is involved with techUK as part of their Cyber People Series, which explores how CISOs should engage at C-Suite and board level, with two reports on the theme released in December 2020 and December 2021.

He has also collaborated with leading analysts firm Kuppinger Cole in Germany, with the Association for Data and Cyber Governance in the US and with the Edutec Alliance in Brazil.

He was listed in the top 10 of UK 30 most influential thought leaders on Risk, RegTech and Compliance by Thomson Reuters in April 2017, and in the top 100 global social media influencers for financial services by Refinitiv in July 2019.

He is a 2022 Onalytica Cybersecurity Influencer, and was also identified by them as 'Social Media Amplifier' on Risk Management in April 2021, and as a 'Key Opinion Leader' on Data Management, IoT Connectivity and RPA in December 2020 and January 2021, as well as an influential voice and subtopic expert on hybrid work and the future of work in January 2022.

He has been ranking consistently in the top 5 of global influencers with Thinkers360 on Cybersecurity, and in the top 10 on Leadership and Management. He was listed as one of their Top Voices for 2023 in October 2023.

He is the author of '*CyberSecurity: The Lost Decade – A Security Governance Handbook for the CISO and the CIO*' first published in September 2017 with updated annual editions released every year up to 2021 (STRF, 2021), and '*The CyberSecurity Leadership Handbook for the CISO and the CEO*' released on Amazon in February 2023 (LeadersPress, 2023).

He produces the Cybersecurity Transformation Podcast on Spotify, an independent podcast with a different take on what's happening in the cybersecurity industry, which entered its fourth series in 2023.

He founded and animates the Security Transformation Research Foundation, a dedicated think tank and research body affiliated to Corix Partners, aimed at approaching Security problems differently and producing innovative and challenging research ideas in the Security, Business Protection, Risk and Controls space.

He is also a Non-Executive Director with Strata Security Solutions and has been a member of the NextWorld Capital European Advisors Network.

Connect with the Author

E: jcgaillard@corixpartners.com
https://www.corixpartners.com/contact
Linkedin: https://www.linkedin.com/in/jcgaillard/
Twitter: @Corix_JC
M: +44 (0)7733 001 530

Acknowledgements

· ·

The content of this book was taken from '*The CyberSecurity Leadership Handbook for the CISO and the CEO*' released on Amazon in February 2023, and other articles published on the Corix Partners blog across 2022 and 2023.

Some of those articles have appeared in Forbes in an edited version, as part of the membership of the author with the Forbes Business Council.

Most articles have been syndicated across a number of websites, including Medium, CIO Water Cooler, and TechNative.io amongst others.

Some parts have been written in collaboration with Vincent Viers (Linkedin: https://www.linkedin.com/in/vincent-viers/).

Many thanks to all – clients, partners, friends – who have been at the heart of this body of work and have contributed to framing the narrative.

References

Boyden. (2016, 09 01). *Cybersecurity: Is Your Board On Board? (Vicky Maxwell Davies).* Retrieved from https://www.linkedin.com/pulse/cybersecurity-your-board-vicky-maxwell-davies/

BT. (2021, 10 12). *CISOs under the spotlight.* Retrieved from https://www.globalservices.bt.com/en/insights/whitepapers/cisos-under-the-spotlight

BusinessWire. (2023, 04 19). *Expel Publishes New Research on the Cybersecurity Challenges Facing British Organisations.* Retrieved from https://www.businesswire.com/news/home/20230419005237/en/Expel-Publishes-New-Research-on-the-Cybersecurity-Challenges-Facing-British-Organisations

CEFCYS. (2020, 01 22). *Je ne porte pas de sweat à capuche, pourtant je travaille dans la cybersécurité.* Récupéré sur https://www.amazon.fr/porte-capuche-pourtant-travaille-cybers%C3%A9curit%C3%A9/dp/2749601622

Cisco. (2019, 03). *Anticipating the Unknowns: CISO Benchmark Study.* Retrieved from https://www.cisco.com/c/dam/m/digital/ elq-cmcglobal/

witb/1963786/2019CISOBenchmarkReportCisco CybersecuritySeries. pdf?ccid=cc000160&dtid=es00tr000875&ecid=14396&oid =wprsc015512

CorixPartners. (2015, 11 19). *The real questions UK Boards should ask following the TalkTalk data breach.* Retrieved from https://corixpartners.com/the-real-questions-uk-boards-should- ask-following-the-talktalk-data-breach-blog/

CorixPartners. (2016, 01 07). *Cyber Security: The Six Questions the Board of Directors Needs to Ask.* Retrieved from https://corixpartners.com/cyber-security-the-six-questions-the-board-of-directors-needs-to-ask/

CorixPartners. (2017, 04 20). *GRC: The 'Three Lines of Defence' model only works on Trust.* Retrieved from https:// corixpartners.com/grc-model-only-works-on-trust/

CorixPartners. (2018, 10 26). *The Digital Transformation and the Role of the CISO.* Retrieved from https://corixpartners.com/ digital-transformation-role-ciso/

CorixPartners. (2018, 04 26). *The tenure of the CISO is key to driving security transformation.* Retrieved from https://corixpartners.com/tenure-ciso-key-driving-security-transformation/

CorixPartners. (2019, 08 22). *Cyber Security: Revisiting the Questions the Board Should Ask.* Retrieved from https:// corixpartners.com/cyber-security-revisiting-board-questions/

CorixPartners. (2020, 01 09). *The Real Leadership Challenges around Cyber Security.* Retrieved from https://corixpartners. com/real-leadership-challenges-cyber-security/

CorixPartners. (2022, 04 14). *Revisiting the questions the Board should ask (one more time...).* Retrieved from https:// corixpartners.com/revisiting-questions-board-should-ask-one-more-time/

DLAPiper. (2023, 01 25). *DLA Piper GDPR Fines and Data Breach Survey: January 2023*. Retrieved from https://www. dlapiper.com/en-ae/insights/publications/2023/01/dla-piper-gdpr-fines-and-data-breach-survey-january-2023

HBR. (2022, 03 04). *7 Pressing Cybersecurity Questions Boards Need to Ask*. Retrieved from https://hbr.org/2022/03/7-pressing-cybersecurity-questions-boards-need-to-ask

HBR. (2023, 04 20). *The Most Successful Approaches to Leading Organizational Change*. Retrieved from https://hbr. org/2023/04/the-most-successful-approaches-to-leading-organizational-change

HelpNetSecurity. (2021, 02 04). *Major trends that are changing the CISO role*. Retrieved from https://www.helpnetsecurity. com/2021/02/04/ciso-responsibilities/

HelpNetSecurity. (2023, 06 22). *Increased spending doesn't translate to improved cybersecurity posture*. Retrieved from https://www.helpnetsecurity.com/2023/06/22/average-cybersecurity-budget-increase/

InfoSecurity. (2021, 05 10). *Interview: Greg Day, Palo Alto Networks on the Changing Role of CISOs* . Retrieved from https://www.infosecurity-magazine.com/interviews/interview-greg-day-palo-alto/

LeadersPress. (2023, 02 21). *The CyberSecurity Leadership Handbook for the CISO and the CEO: How to Fix Decade-Old Issues and Protect Your Organization from Cyber Threats*. Retrieved from https://www.amazon.com/dp/B0BW51C5J1/

McKinsey. (2019, 10 08). *The risk-based approach to cybersecurity*. Retrieved from https://www.mckinsey.com/capabilities/risk-and-resilience/our-insights/the-risk-based-approach-to-cybersecurity.

McKinsey. (2021, 08 4). *Organizational cyber maturity: A survey of industries*. Retrieved from https://www.mckinsey.com/capabilities/risk-and-resilience/our-insights/organizational-cyber-maturity-a-survey-of-industries

McKinsey. (2023, 03 15). *Actions the best CEOs are taking in 2023*. Retrieved from https://www.mckinsey.com/capabilities/strategy-and-corporate-finance/our-insights/actions-the-best-ceos-are-taking-in-2023

Nominet. (2020). *CISO STRESS: Life Inside the Perimeter: One Year On*. Retrieved from https://media.nominetcyber.com/wp-content/uploads/2020/02/Nominet_The-CISO-Stress-Report_2020_V10.pdf

STRF. (2019). *Cyber Security: A Look Across Two Decades*. Retrieved from https://securitytransformation.com/wp-content/uploads/2017/07/CyberSecurity-A-Look-Across-2-Decades-FINAL1-19SEP2019.pdf

STRF. (2021). *Cyber Security: The Lost Decade – 2021 Edition*. Retrieved from https://www.blurb.co.uk/b/10807892-cyber-security-the-lost-decade-2021-edition

techUK. (2021, 12 02). *techUK sets out recommendations to help guide CISOs as organisations continue their digital transformation*. Retrieved from https://www.techuk.org/resource/techuk-sets-out-recommendations-to-help-guide-cisos-as-organisations-continue-their-digital-transformation.html

TrendMicro. (2021, 10 12). *Cybersecurity Tool Sprawl Drives Plans to Outsource Detection and Response*. Retrieved from https://newsroom.trendmicro.com/2021-10-12-Cybersecurity-Tool-Sprawl-Drives-Plans-to-Outsource-Detection-and-Response

WEF. (2019, 10 25). *The Cybersecurity Guide for Leaders in Today's Digital World* . Retrieved from https://www.weforum.org/reports/the-cybersecurity-guide-for-leaders-in-today-s-digital-world

WEF. (2020, 05 26). *Cybersecurity Leadership Principles: Lessons learnt during the COVID-19 pandemic to prepare for the new normal* . Retrieved from https://www.weforum.org/reports/cybersecurity-leadership-principles-lessons-learnt-during-the-covid-19-pandemic-to-prepare-for-the-new-normal

ZDNet. (2020, 02 12). *Average tenure of a CISO is just 26 months due to high stress and burnout* . Retrieved from https://www.zdnet.com/article/average-tenure-of-a-ciso-is-just-26-months-due-to-high-stress-and-burnout/